"David is a living demonstration of peace and joy. He uncovered this state of mind, which is accessible to us all, by living what he teaches in *This Moment Is Your Miracle*. Although the process of transcending fear is not always easy, it *is* simple, and David's explanations and exercises guide you to claim the happiness that is your birthright. *This Moment Is Your Miracle* illuminates the pathway to complete awakening, so you can experience the deep peace and everlasting love that dwells within you, in this very moment."

—**Corinne Zupko, EdS**, bestselling author of
From Anxiety to Love

"It is said, 'By their fruits ye shall know them'; this book is the harvest of all the teachings that David Hoffmeister has acquired during the learning and living of *A Course in Miracles*. The joy of David is his trust, his willingness to give freely, and his simple practice of listening to the Holy Spirit and following His directions. The resulting inspiration of this book is due to the experience of direct communion with the Spirit, and consequently is a blessing to all who want to live a life of forgiveness and healing."

—**Nick Davis**, founder of the first UK-dedicated Miracles
Centre, The Centre for Inner Peace, and the retreat,
September Cottage; author of *An Invitation to the
Awakening Heart*

"David Hoffmeister is one of the most authentic teachers of *A Course in Miracles*. His commitment to the text comes through in all of his work. I love David's gentle teaching style and his genuine love for life. David walks his talk!"

—**Gabrielle Bernstein**, #1 Nev
of *The Universe Has Your Ba*

"'Imagine if you were motivated only by love and nothing else?' asks David Hoffmeister in his new book, packed with detailed explanations, practices, prayers, and recorded meditations. David unpacks *A Course in Miracles* in bite-sized pieces about how to undo the mind and pump up the volume of Holy Spirit. Dive deep into this book and you will experience your miracle-mindedness strengthen as you practice the core teachings of *A Course in Miracles*. Move over Ego, we are merging into the 'Glorious Flow'!"

> —**Maria Felipe**, author of *Live Your Happy*, international speaker of *A Course in Miracles*, and ordained minister through Pathways of Light

"I've known David for nearly thirty years. There are several folks who have dedicated themselves to understanding and living the principle of *A Course in Miracles*. In the case of David, it's clear that his commitment is strong, his vision is sharp, and his ability to teach brilliant. *This Moment Is Your Miracle* is a well-written, comprehensive explanation of some of the most basic, revolutionary, and transformative concepts in the Course."

> —**Jon Mundy, PhD**, author of *Living A Course in Miracles*, publisher of *Miracles* magazine, and executive director of All Faiths Seminary in New York City, NY

"With his new book, *This Moment is Your Miracle*, David Hoffmeister gives the reader a tour de force of spiritual knowledge that will result in a major acceleration of their spiritual path. I've known David for many years, and he's a brilliant teacher and writer. This book shows him at his best. I highly recommend this important work."

> —**Gary Renard**, the best-selling author of *The Disappearance of the Universe* trilogy and *The Lifetimes When Jesus and Buddha Knew Each Other*

"The journey within is the greatest journey of all. David Hoffmeister takes us through a journey of self-discovery, inner truth, healing, and rebirth.... David gives us the tools to face our fears.... I recommend *This Moment Is Your Miracle* for anyone wanting to take the greatest journey of all."

—**Tina Fiorda**, coauthor of *A Book of Insight*

"For both new and seasoned travelers on the path to self-discovery, this book is filled to the brim with a wealth of inspiring, practical material that can lead you straight to the heart of deep inner peace. These abundant, essential reminders about the constant and powerful choice for beginning anew are presented in a bright, masterful, and compelling way. More than ever, this easy, loving way of living will now feel within reach, and you can eagerly begin to claim your birthright!"

—**Carol Howe**, author of *Never Forget to Laugh*

"*This Moment Is Your Miracle* brings the luminous love and transforming clarity contained within *A Course in Miracles* alive for a new generation of seekers. With eloquence and grounded wisdom, David shows us that miracles are not only possible, but natural and abundantly available to us all."

—**Miranda MacPherson**, author of *The Way of Grace*

"David Hoffmeister is a master teacher when it comes to understanding the profoundly healing spiritual practices in *A Course in Miracles*. David shares simple, step-by-step healing practices that correct the mind and liberate us from the dominion of the ego's false concepts and precepts. *A Course in Miracles* readers can be deceived into thinking that studying the books will bring healing, but healing is not an intellectual process, it is a spiritual awakening. With this book, we're given the practical tips and tools that bring us to that awakening. This helpful book is a master's guide to practicing *A Course in Miracles* and living the teachings moment by moment for true liberation."

—**Jennifer Hadley**, spiritual writer, speaker, teacher, minister, and counselor; founder of the *Power of Love Ministry*

"*This Moment Is Your Miracle* is a heartwarming and heart-opening read. It creates a sense of shelter and safety, navigating you through practical exercises that show you God within and all around you. You are invited to trust love. You are shown how to heal obstacles such as fear and guilt. This book prepares you to surrender to love. There are clear explanations of how life has distracted your attention, taking you from the flow of love. This book is an invitation to recognize your oneness with God and with the Holy Spirit. It offers intimacy with pure love, for those who have the heart for it."

—**Jac O'Keeffe**, spiritual teacher, author, and cofounder of the Association of Professional Spiritual Teachers (APST)

THIS MOMENT IS YOUR MIRACLE

Spiritual Tools to Transcend Fear
and Experience the Power
of the Present Moment

DAVID HOFFMEISTER

REVEAL PRESS

AN IMPRINT OF NEW HARBINGER PUBLICATIONS

Publisher's Note

This publication is designed to provide accurate and authoritative information in regard to the subject matter covered. It is sold with the understanding that the publisher is not engaged in rendering psychological, financial, legal, or other professional services. If expert assistance or counseling is needed, the services of a competent professional should be sought.

Library of Congress Cataloging-in-Publication Data on file

21   20   19

10   9   8   7   6   5   4   3   2

This book is dedicated to the group of people I have lived with for years who have dedicated their lives to experiencing the truth within: Living Miracles Worldwide Spiritual Community. I am honored by your dedication and devotion and touched by your kindness and generosity. There are no words to adequately express my gratitude.

Love is completely transparent; it's an open book.

CONTENTS

Part IV: Being the Miracle

FOREWORD

It is easy to talk about spiritual ideas, harder to live them. When a spiritual teacher comes along who actually walks the talk, all who look upon that person are blessed with a rare opportunity to learn, heal, and grow. David Hoffmeister is such a one.

When I discovered David through his YouTube videos, I was deeply impressed by his clarity, authenticity, sense of purpose, and ease. He is authoritative and consistent. David has devoted his life to proving and teaching the principles of A Course in Miracles. I have been with the Course about as long as David has. Still, I encounter fear, resistance, and ego. David has been a huge inspiration and accelerator to my advancement in the Course, through his impeccable understanding and, most important, his model. If you sincerely intend to master A Course in Miracles or any related spiritual path, David is a guide of the highest caliber.

A Course in Miracles is a delight to the spirit, but a huge confrontation to the ego. It pulls the rug out from under the ego's tricks and exposes it for the nothingness it is. For that reason, all students of the Course experience resistance to the program. Many students quit doing the lessons, and others complain, "I don't understand the text." Yet, the very same students admit, "I know the Course contains truths that can change my life. I just wish it were easier to apply."

The book you are holding can help you do exactly that. Here is a brilliant map of the journey from fear to love. David takes the essential principles of the Course and breaks them down into easy-to-grasp ideas, exercises, and steps to help you make the truths work in your life. David can take you where you want to go because he has walked the path you and I now walk. He knows where the open road is and where lurk the pitfalls that may waylay us. Read, learn, open, awaken, and transform.

In one of David's teachings, he mentions that Mahatma Gandhi retained his peace of mind even while he was in prison. The revered leader did some of his best writing there. The lesson David extracts is that it is not what our body is doing that makes us happy or miserable, but where our mind is. Hearing that, I remembered a prisoner I used to visit. While Ray was in college, he flew into a fit of rage and beat his girlfriend. A few days later, she died. Ray was convicted of manslaughter and sentenced to many years in jail. I met Ray during his ninth year of incarceration, when he came up for parole for the third time. "My girlfriend's parents are wealthy and politically influential people," he told me. "Every year when I come up for parole, they wage an intensive campaign to 'keep this vicious killer off the streets.' So far, they have been successful, and I have been denied parole."

I didn't see a vicious killer before me. To the contrary, the Ray I knew was a gentle, kind man, penitent for his tragic mistake. He was a model prisoner, given the highest privileges and appointed manager of the prison laundry. He was a devoted student of A Course in Miracles. He was peaceful, his heart was open, and he displayed an exemplary disposition.

Ray's attitude and that of his girlfriend's parents were a great teaching for me. His body was in prison, but his spirit was soaring. That couple had all the material amenities and physical freedom anyone could desire, but their hearts were consumed with hatred and revenge. Who was really in prison?

After walking the spiritual path for many years, I have observed two kinds of seminars: One kind teaches us how to get stuff. The other kind teaches us how to get free. David's teachings are among the best of the latter.

When I met David, I told him that I watch his YouTube videos and read his books before I go to sleep each night. Immersing myself in his ideas and consciousness is a soothing, healing way to undo the tangles of the day and segue into a peaceful night's sleep. David's teachings can achieve the same for you, day or night. I count this man as one of the great blessings in my life.

When climbing a mountain in India, Sherpas (guides) help you ascend. One Sherpa takes you to a certain altitude, and then another Sherpa guides you to the next level. So it is with life. We are graced to have guides show us the way when we feel lost or confused. David Hoffmeister is a Sherpa of immaculate purpose. Trust him. He can show you the way to the mountaintop.

—Alan Cohen

THE EVER-PRESENT MIRACLE OF NOW

All we need to do is go within to find the answer of love.

There is an answer that is so deep that it can bring truth and healing to everyone and to this whole world. We have been searching for it everywhere, except in the only place we could truly find it: within.

This moment extends all the way to eternity. It is the now that extends peacefully and is forever and ever. It is infinite happiness, without end, without limit. It is untouched by fear, guilt, or suffering of any kind. It is untouched by anything but love. There is so much appreciation when experiencing something for the first time. There is no comparison. For in the ever-unfolding now, *we* are always brand new. We can just bask in it, fully merge with it. There are no past references to it, for it doesn't fit on the timeline. It's just a happy sense of soaring way beyond time and space, like an ongoing meditation.

This ever-present miracle of now is our doorway within. It is our doorway Home. It is an experience of something ever-new. It's a happy feeling, one that makes you want to sing to the world. It's very beautiful and very simple too. It's having the allowance to merge when you are watching a flower, a butterfly, or a bird singing in the tree; it's a contentment like, "Ah yes, thank you; let me be whole." This is what Saint Francis was talking about: just communing. The allowance that everything is perfect. We can really allow ourselves to smell the roses.

It is through the doorway of the present moment that we are truly able to hear the deep messages of love coming from within. They are boundless and eternal, for the voice of the inner guide is always speaking to us of our true identity and of our oneness with everyone and everything. But in order to hear it, we need to walk through the doorway and invite this deeply loving guide into our minds and lives.

I first knew about this present moment, where boundless joy resides, early on. The true drive of my heart, even as a young boy, was to feel joy and extend love. I remember playing all summer. I loved the neighborhood creek, which was full of frogs and crawdads. I would just play, play, play—play my heart out all day. I was truly in the moment, naturally!

Then, as I got older and the world's rules and expectations set in, I bought the bait. I started thinking that I had to learn my way through this world. However, the more intricate the education and learning, the more confused and lost I became. I didn't like the idea of "improving" and the sound of "making a living." It sounded like pressure, like living to just survive. That was not inspiring. It felt like the world was set up with an ever-increasing number of complications. There came a time when I began to question all this; I questioned how it was all set up.

I started seeking the answer when I got into graduate school. I began to question everything that I believed and everything I had learned in my ten years of university. Even though I got a couple of degrees, I soon realized that there was no point in learning more stuff and developing more special skills. I wanted the answer to something deeper. This was definitely not popular with people in my life. They said, "No, no, not good, you have no direction; you are going to amount to nothing." They would say things like, "You are crazy, get a life."

So, I would say, "Okay, let's talk about that. Get a life: Can you be a little more specific? I actually believe I am going for life. So, would you tell me what you mean by *get a life?*"

They said, "Well, get a life: a girlfriend, a partner...something. Then get a house, get a mortgage, get in debt like the rest of us."

"That is what you mean by get a life? And then what?"

And they said, "And then you grow old, and your hair goes gray."

"And then what?"

"And then you get sick."

"And then what?"

"And then you die."

And I said, "Absolutely unacceptable. All I can say is, if that is your definition of a life, I am not going to get a life. There has to be something more than just struggle and work and suffer and get sick and die and get educated along the way. There has to be a little bit more than that, a deeper and more fulfilling experience. And I am going to get the bottom of it; I am going to get to the bottom of this fishy world, and I am going to find out what is truly possible."

When *A Course in Miracles* finally came along for me in 1986, I opened it up and almost lost my breath. I felt like a lot of people do: that it was really, really powerful. Something inside of me said, "*Ahhh....* Support!" It was such a powerful wayshower. It was like a guide. There was an inner voice urging me, "Keep it up. Don't stop now. You are on the road to truth. You are coming inward with all this deep questioning. Keep going." The journey that followed can be summed up as a love affair with God. I never planned my life to unfold that way. And I certainly did not grow up consciously thinking that this was how I wanted to spend my life.

After several years of reading *A Course in Miracles*, I began to hear the voice of the inner guide. This quiet voice was giving me very helpful and often very specific instructions on where to go, what to say, and what to do. I no longer had to navigate through this maze of a world on my own anymore! Listening to and following this voice seemed to assure my peace and happiness. My prayer had been answered! I had an inner guide who was there to answer any question and help me make every decision. It was an amazing gift and a tremendous relief!

Nowadays, I spend most of my time meeting people like you who are looking for happiness and a deeper sense of purpose in their lives. And time and time again, people all over the world ask me the *how* questions: How do I find true peace? How do I find true happiness? How do I find the quiet peace, the kind of peace and happiness that will last? I have taught on six continents and in forty-four countries, and no matter where I go, people always ask me, *How, How, How?*

And this is what I say: "By unveiling and forgiving your blocks to love."

And then they ask: "But how do I forgive? How do I let go of fear? How do I heal and come to peace of mind? Can you give me a practical formula? Can you give me something that I can use every day?"

There is nothing more fun to me than giving the *how* away—and that is my intention with this book. Once you experience it, you feel how wonderful it is, and then you will want to give it away too.

The bottom line of the *how* is: Make contact with Holy Spirit, with God, with the Higher Self, whatever you prefer to call it. Once you connect with Spirit—which I call Holy Spirit—you are in direct contact with the how, for the Holy Spirit is the how. You are right there in the moment with the how, experiencing it moving through you.

It is in the power of this moment where the how resides. It is only now that we are truly able to forgive and move from a fearful state into a loving one. It is only in this moment that we are truly able to experience the miracle of letting every dark thought and feeling and every pain and suffering go, shined away by the Holy Spirit. It is only in this moment that we are truly able to perform the miracle of forgiveness. The miracle of this moment is always available, ready to take us beyond the intellect and back into an experience of pure love and of our true divine nature.

Forgiveness—the process of seeing no problems—offers a doorway into the intuitive flow of presence and the ability to just ride that presence like a feather floating on the breeze. Presence with the Holy Spirit brings us to a place where there are no difficult decisions, for the Spirit is always out in front of us, showing us the way. There is no hesitation or doubt, just an increasingly consistent sense of relaxation and ease. When we have contact with Spirit, with our internal teacher, and this contact becomes consistent, the ease comes into our life.

The primary aim of this book is to help you come into the flow of the present moment where you can hear the voice of the Holy Spirit. The Holy Spirit, the ever-present comforter and guide, is always there in the quiet depths of your mind, waiting for you to come with your prayers, with your offerings of forgiveness, and with your requests for guidance. The Holy Spirit is always there to help you let go of what you no longer want and to help you unwind from your faulty perception of the world—a fragmented perception that tells you that you are separate from the unifying love at your core, the love that you are.

If you truly want to experience a lasting sense of peace and happiness and of love and joy, and want to save time getting there, I would like to offer you a spirituality that is *very* practical. In my experience, it comes down to the formula of 1 percent principle and 99 percent practice. The 1 percent principle must be truly helpful, leading you out of the illusion of separation and not deeper into it. At the end of the day, focusing much more on the practice of forgiveness rather than on the theory is the fast track to true peace and happiness. The consistent practical application of true principle is what makes lasting change.

To help you do this, I am going to take you on a journey deep within. It's a journey of self-inquiry and self-discovery that makes change possible. Without going within, studying your own mind, and taking a good close look at the false thoughts and beliefs you have about yourself, you cannot find the answers and change you are looking for. Throughout the book, I will use the terms "Holy Spirit" and "ego" as if they are separate, autonomous powers. This way of communicating about the two different thought systems in our mind has a purpose: to acknowledge that the ego-thought system is separate from God. The ego-thought system, which is separate from your true Self, comes from a false belief in fear, guilt, and sacrifice. It is behind every doubt, every feeling of littleness, and every wish for separation. The Holy Spirit's thought system, on the other hand, is something we are relearning to think and operate from, bridging the gap of separation in our disconnected hearts and minds and allowing us to remember our true identity as Divine Spirit.

The only way out of the ego-thought system is through the doorway of the moment, this *miracle moment* that is untouched by any past association or future anticipation. Yet, to live in an experience of the present moment, we must become aware of and expose our unconscious beliefs. We need to expose the ego fully, which is nothing more than a voice of fear and doubt. It is important not to be hard on ourselves when we fall into the ego's doubt trap, for here lies our opportunity to raise the ego into awareness. And it is only by becoming aware of the ego that it can be seen for what it is and then forgiven in the light of the Holy Spirit. We cannot really judge our advances from our retreats. In fact, we cannot conclude anything as we go through this transformation. So, be gentle with yourself as you allow the darkness to rise into your awareness to be released.

As you start to release the attack thoughts, grievances, and judgments that come up, the world will slowly start to light up. You will start to see more and more loving reflections. And though it may seem like there is more light in the world, it is really your mind that is filling with light again. A devoted practice of bringing all your dark thoughts and feelings to the light will result in revelations of evermore light and love filling your mind. The exposure of the ego is an ongoing and necessary process that precedes the complete joining with the Holy Spirit. With your willingness, this book will help you take the beginning steps toward this most glorious experience of becoming happy, becoming at peace, and finding your true purpose.

The Holy Spirit's answer to all of the world's seeming complexities and choices is the miracle. In A Course in Miracles, the "miracle" is defined as a change of perception from fear to love. Although there are steps involved, with practice, all thoughts of conflict and suffering are easily raised into the Spirit's light and released to free the mind to experience the miracle. The miracle is never out there, in the future. It is always right here, in the present. It's merely been covered by the doubt and fear generated by our mistaken belief that we are separate from God.

The journey within leads us beyond the intellect and into an experience of pure love, which is our true nature! In order to experience that feeling of love consistently, however, we have to go through an experiential purification and transformation process. And it's interesting that the word "course" is in the title because at some point when you're reading A Course in Miracles, it begins to dawn on you that this course is asking you to unlearn absolutely everything that is unlike your true nature. So, instead of "doing" a course and "learning" something new, your mind is being emptied of everything it has ever learned about itself and the world, which has nothing to do with who you really are.

This is why we need mind training. Mind training is training ourselves to think with Spirit again, with love again, with God again. Mind training makes the unconscious mind conscious. I call the unconscious mind "the unwatched mind," for it is constantly wandering and distracting us from remembering our true identity. When the mind wanders into an ego trap, it's very important to come back to the present moment and the sense of peace it brings. The practical spiritual path is a practice of finding and tapping into the Holy Spirit's thought system of freedom and following it carefully. The practical tools I offer you throughout this book will support you in finding and establishing this thought system.

Sometimes people ask me if they need to love the ego. We can't love the ego since the ego is the belief that there is no love. We can't love something that is the total denial of love! The ego doesn't really exist since it is just a belief. So, we are not trying to heal or awaken the ego. That is impossible. Self-improvement does not solve anything. The Self that God created does not need to be improved; it is already perfect. What you can do is expose your ego beliefs, raise them to the light of the Holy Spirit, and then watch them disappear. This is how you see that the ego wasn't real, and you can have a good belly laugh at it.

Until our belief system is deeply examined, the ego will continue to have a grip on us. It has control over our roles and responsibilities. It has control over almost everything we do and say. Until we have examined our mind deeply enough to allow Spirit to use our roles and responsibilities for a loving purpose, the ego will use them for its own ends. There is nothing in between: you either let your mind be used by the Spirit or by the ego. By giving over the roles and responsibilities to the Holy Spirit, they can be repurposed for the Spirit's healing of your mind. Your career, hobbies, talents, and relationships can all be used in miraculous ways you never dreamed were possible. I've marveled as I watched all the skills that I had developed be used in completely new and different ways by the Holy Spirit. The practicality of it is amazing. It is like the unwinding action of turning a screw out of a wall. The ego has really wound us into this belief system, and that's why it takes many gentle turns to come out of it.

I am very excited to start this journey with you. When I meet someone, it is never a fleeting encounter. We are here to truly bless each other's lives, to be of full support to one another. I feel like I am always meeting my beloved Self. We have a lifelong link; we have a lifelong connection of awakening to truth together. Even though our bodies seem to be in different parts of the world, we have a communication link. We can join together through the power of thought, through the power of prayer, and through Spirit. It is in our hearts.

The result of this journey is profound beyond imagination. In spiritual practice, like any other practice, the more you put in, the more you will get out. Willingness goes a very, very long way! The tools I will give you can help you see that the sticky and painful aspects of your everyday life can ultimately be the springboards to a sustained experience of profound freedom and joy.

If you have a strong desire to know your beloved Self, know that the feeling is mutual and that joining together in this unified purpose is more profound than you might think. Let's begin.

PART I

THE MIRACLE OF

MOVING THROUGH

SEPARATION

CHAPTER 1

JUDGMENT AND KNOWLEDGE

One time I was walking with a friend when she spontaneously burst into laughter and said, "You have a butterfly on your butt!" I looked back, and, sure enough, there was a butterfly getting a free lift on my backside. I said, "Okay. Enjoy the ride!" We continued to walk down the road, and it dawned on me that the butterfly would be more comfortable riding on my finger. So, I put my index finger in the air and told my friend that I was going to call the butterfly to ride on my finger. She was all for it. I called to it telepathically, "Come on up. There is a great view here. The butt is okay, but you'll like it up here. You can be like a little hood ornament." And it did! It flew around, landed on my finger, and stayed there with its little antennae out. Of course, my friend laughed even harder. It was a fun walk, with the butterfly symbolizing our innocence.

Like children, animals respond to defenselessness. When you are meek, joyful, and innocent, you draw forth many reflections. At our monastery, the chipmunks come right up our legs. It is like a Saint Francis moment. Everything we see is innocent. I see this truth in people and events. I am into not seeing error. I am into seeing innocence everywhere and in everyone. This is why people and animals, and even butterflies, want to be near me. When the mind is whole and not split, you see only innocence, and you feel happy and loving all the time!

The Split

Imagine for a second an awake mind. This mind is used to the wholeness, sameness, and constancy of Heaven's oneness. Suddenly, a doubt thought seems to arise. Now the mind has two irreconcilable thought systems—one of love and one of fear. The tension from trying to hold this split together is intolerable since the two thought systems have no meeting point and are total opposites of each other. Therefore, the mind attempts to see the split outside instead of within, where it was conceived. Thus, a world of duality and opposites is made: a place with opposing views and changing desires.

The ego says, "I know how you can alleviate this terrible tension: just get rid of your feelings of pain and guilt by projecting them out onto the world." This is how pain, fear, doubt, and sorrow became the common experience of this world. This is how the mind made a world of duality, of up and down, of good and bad, and of right and wrong. The only reason we seem to experience health and sickness, war and peace, life and death, and all the variations, degrees, and extremes is simply judgment. That is the trick of this world. Whenever we judge or condemn, the mind is projecting, and says, "That person, thing, or situation out there is at fault." It does this to cover the guilt of the separation from God, which, believe it or not, is at the core of every conceived problem in this world. It makes the world into a smokescreen as it thinks it can be free of the guilt by putting it outside, while believing it is actually within. It is only by believing there is darkness within that our mind would ever attempt to project it outside.

How Good Is Good Enough?

Growing up in this world, there is a lot of pressure and high expectations to do something constructive, develop skills, and gain special knowledge to develop a life skill for self-sufficiency. We're told that it's important to get higher and higher degrees and accumulate more and more special knowledge. This is stressful, and it's coming from a strong cultural belief in personal responsibility, which has, at its core, a sense of guilt. It's built in to the system, and it seems noble and good, yet the pressure for self-reliance is hurting us.

Not many can escape the questions running in the back of our minds: *How good is good enough? Did I do enough? Did I fulfill obligations? Did I live up to standards?* The ego sets us up to be forever stressed-out, always thinking that there is something we could change or make better. This is rigid learned behavior, but another perspective is available, a perfectly different and perfectly gentle means and perspective.

A Course in Miracles says, "In no situation that arises do you realize the outcome that would make you happy." Not in some—in none! But you're not left hanging; the next lesson states, "Everything is for your own best interests." Everything! This can feel just as shocking as the first message.

All things work together for good with no exceptions except in the ego's judgment. Talk about undoing the analytical mind! Suddenly, there's no point in trying to analyze or judge anything. What a relief!

Our Deepest Problem

The deepest problem that we have is the thinking, the stereotyping, the breaking-things-apart mechanism. I call this the "I-know" egoic mind. The ego is always fragmented; it made up a fragmented world, and it's always categorizing, analyzing, diagnosing, and fixing things. It's very much a dysfunctional thought system, based on the myth of separation.

In the traditional Genesis story, God said to Adam and Eve, "Don't eat from the tree of the knowledge of good and evil." But the serpent lured Eve into taking an apple, and she gave one to Adam. Then, according to biblical myth, they were kicked out of the Garden of Eden. This is the fall from grace—the separation from God after which a lot of darkness and fear arose in the mind, reflected in the form of wars, division in religions, and all kinds of insane pursuits. The exercise of religions is largely an attempt to find a way to return to God's love through ritual and tradition.

I would like to propose a different path than ritual and tradition, a different story about a God that didn't kick anyone out. We can call this the metaphysical take on the traditional story: let Adam and Eve represent you and I, and in this story, we never left God. And he never abandoned us. Here, the "fall" is nothing more than a perceptual distortion, a vast illusion in which the mind *believed* that it pulled off something that in reality is impossible: separation from an all-knowing, all-loving creator.

We have very powerful minds that are capable of imagining, or "thinking up," this whole universe. In my revision of Genesis, there was no apple. We simply asked a question: Could there be anything more than Heaven or oneness, more than everything? This question was like a little puff of madness since "more than everything," more than perfect love and harmony, is of course completely impossible. Imagine this idea, this question, or this doubt thought as one of those little white dandelion puffs blowing across the road. This powerful mind of ours allowed the thought, this puff, to spread. It was of course a totally ludicrous idea, but instead of laughing it away with our all-powerful, divine mind, we took it seriously. Taking this puff of an idea seriously made us forget the truth that we have everything and are one with God. We closed ourselves off and started dreaming we were a tiny part of an impossible world. Many people ask me how this could happen if our mind is part of God's and if we are divine. The truth is, it didn't happen apart from our belief, and there's a true knowing or awareness of this once all our false beliefs are questioned and released.

> Into eternity, where all is one, there crept a tiny, mad idea, at which the Son of God remembered not to laugh. In his forgetting did the thought become a serious idea, and possible of both accomplishment and real effects. Together, we can laugh them both away, and understand that time cannot intrude upon eternity. It is a joke to think that time can come to circumvent eternity, which means there is no time....
>
> It is reasonable to ask how the mind could ever have made the ego. In fact, it is the best question you could ask. There is, however, no point in giving an answer in terms of the past because the past does not matter, and history would not exist if the same errors were not being repeated in the present.

The Answer to a World of Duality

Many mystics call this the world of duality. This is what the story of Adam and Eve and the Garden of Eden builds for us. Adam and Eve wanted to hide in the Garden, so they covered themselves and their "private parts" with fig leaves. They felt guilt and shame for what they had done. By way of this analogy, at the moment of the fall or separation, because the guilt feels so awful, the mind projects this guilt out as the time-space cosmos, which then becomes like a giant fig leaf under which the mind tries to hide from its creator. The mind wants to hide what it believes are its private thoughts because it's terrified of God's love, so it makes a fake identity, the persona.

God is pure love and oneness. He has no awareness of separation; thus, He cannot come into duality. The world of duality is the illusory hiding place for the sleeping mind that believes it has separated from God. To this mind, the ego says: "Here is your new home now. Be content with the body and the world as your new home. We will make up every-thing that you seemed to have in oneness. We will make a new kind of love with bodies. We will make a new kind of freedom with movement of bodies. We will make a new kind of happiness with pleasures of the senses to take the place of your Home in Heaven. And God cannot come in and find you here, you will have privacy, and you can do anything that you want." This is how the body became the central focus for the ego.

The ego wants God to bless its new world and give reality to the fantasy of time and space. There is an anger deep down in the mind because God cannot do this. God cannot give reality to a projected dream of form! God is divine love. God knows you only as divine love. This love is abstract light, total joy, constant communication, and peace. It is infinite and perfect. God would not be God if He granted the ego's wish to give this world reality. Therefore, all anger is a temper tantrum based on a desire for the temporary to be true and real. Ego tries to lure you to think that you are free in a world of form, but it doesn't tell you that it, the ego, is the ruler. It thinks that as long as you are busy plan-ning for the future, dreaming of a better form (or lamenting the past), you won't think about God and the oneness that is your true identity.

This is showing you that the ego is a thought system in your mind that doesn't lead you into a true experience of who you are. It only makes sure you stay preoccupied in the world of form, in time and space.

So, once the mind fell asleep and started to dream of separation, it was like a nightmare at first since God and Heaven were completely pushed out of awareness. It was a deep sleep of forgetfulness, and there were suddenly two thought systems instead of one. One was the fear-based thought system of the ego, the "puff," and the other was the thought system of God's loving answer, the Holy Spirit. The ego's thought system, based on the premise that an impossible separation happened, says, "If you ever go back into your mind, and into that white light, God will get you and destroy you!" This creates a perpetual neurotic state that compels the mind to constantly seek for answers and safety where they can't be found: in the projected forms of this world. But in the stillness, at the core of our being, the loving answer just keeps reminding us, "You never left. You never could have separated. God is not angry at you! Your Father loves you! Your Father will always love you!"

We can't solve our problems with the same level of thinking that created them. We can't find the solution at the level of the problem, at the level of separation; the answer has to be a higher order thinking that lifts us up and back into harmony. You cannot approach a solution with the sleeping mind since this was the mind that believed in the problem in the first place. You have to rise above the level of the problem, above where the problem is perceived, to find the answer. You have a perceptual problem, and as long as you try to make things better and fix things at the level of the ego, you're not going anywhere. You're just spinning your wheels like a hamster going round and round, and there's no progress whatsoever. You are more like the scarecrow in *The Wizard of Oz*, where all of your straw is scattered all over the road. But when you let go of compartmentalizing, categorizing, labeling, and ordering everything, you find yourself coming into peace. You find yourself identifying with your true Self and not with a separate identity. The peace that you find is a state of mind in which you perceive that everything is perfect, it has always been perfect, and nothing has been out of order. Your mind just needs some training to reach this awareness.

Leaping into Spirit's Perception

The fall from grace, the separation, which is an idea in the mind and not a point on the timeline, didn't leave us forever lost and without an answer. At the moment of that tiny mad idea—the separation—God gave an immediate answer. Being all-knowing love, He answered this doubt thought, this tiny mad idea, this "puff," with the awareness that this never happened, that it is impossible. We can call this answer the Holy Spirit. The Holy Spirit can be referred to as the still, small voice within the mind, or the intuition, that guides us. It's like a presence that we can sense whenever we get still enough to tune in and listen inwardly. We need to know this and also become aware of how easily defenses like judgment, worldly knowledge, denial, and repression are used to dilute the terror and prevent us from experiencing God's answer.

We don't go from analysis and judgment into perfection without a willingness to say, "Show me Holy Spirit; I need to be shown." Even in moments when you're upset with God, with life, or with the way you perceive the situations you're involved in, you need to be willing to perceive things differently and open up to relying on the Spirit's healed perception.

You need help to truly see another world than the one you projected from your ego's fear and doubt and worry. You can freely say, "You need to convince me," and throw it all back to the Holy Spirit. Ask to be shown. Let it be a convincing job for the multitude of angels cheering every time you make a movement toward trusting your intuition. That should catch your attention and turn you toward the miracle in your mind. You need the Holy Spirit's help to see things as they are, to see clearly without projection, judgment, and interpretation.

As soon as the ego judges somebody else as lacking, it always compares and tells you, "Well, *you* are not that way; you are beyond that." This promotes inequality, division, and separation. You need to ask the Holy Spirit to start cleaning the filter you are seeing through because that is the only hope you have of truly not judging. Once you tap in to that help, it is delightful. Every moment without a filter is delightful. But if there is a concept or a judgment involved, then it is better to just pause, introspect, and become aware of what that filter is. You can cultivate a willingness to question every value and every concept you hold. When you catch yourself judging or thinking that you know something, I advise you to exercise what I call, "stop, drop, and roll." You first pause your running thoughts and your reactions; you stop! And second, you exercise your willingness to drop it. And third, you roll with the Spirit's guidance.

When your filter starts clearing and the more intuitive and less judging you become, the more you reap the emotional benefits. You can tell by how you feel: you're more stable, you're calmer, and this is how you know you're headed in the right direction. This develops into acceptance and a receptive mind, an open mind, a mind that doesn't "already know." Then the miracle within can happen.

It's normal in this world to encourage opinions, but opinions block the experience of peace. Opinions do not have anything to do with truth or reality. The "I-don't-know" state is humble. In the Zen tradition, it is called beginner's mind. It is a great experience to wake up every day and feel like you don't know anything. It's a beautiful feeling to not have an opinion but to be open to be shown.

EXERCISE: Moving from Opinions to Prayer

Spend one day observing the I-know mind and try spending it without one single opinion. Try it out! Get the flavor of it. As you go through your day, ask yourself, "Where is my mind when I am caught up in my opinions, thinking I know something, and how do I feel when I am open and I do not think I already know the answers?"

Throughout your day, notice how many times you:

- think you know the answer to something

- want to know the answer

- say or think opinionated statements

- make assumptions about someone or something

- interrupt a conversation because you think you know better than someone

- do something solely based on past outcomes and past learning

After your practice day of having no opinions, spend some time reflecting in your journal. Find a quiet place where you won't be disturbed. Close your eyes, take a few deep breaths, relax, and allow your mind to get still for a few minutes. Then, read the following questions slowly. Reflect and write down your answers. Allow yourself to have an experience of the answer—go beyond the intellect.

1. Has my way, my own "knowledge," brought me to a state of consistent peace and happiness?

2. Seeing that my "knowledge" or choices have not yet led me to a state of consistent peace and happiness, am I willing to open to the possibility of another way?

3. In releasing my I-know mind, am I willing to trust that there is a wisdom, a Holy Spirit, within my mind, that has my best interests and my highest good in His hands?

4. Do I trust that He knows what I need?

5. Can I trust that He knows the prayer (desire) of my heart and that He will bring to me what is truly most helpful for my healing and therefore my happiness?

If any of your answers to questions two through five is no, there is a line in *A Course in Miracles* that can help ease your mind. It states that if you find resistance strong and dedication weak, you should not fight yourself. Be gentle with yourself and give yourself permission to pray for help with any areas or patterns you've noticed. Acknowledgment of where you are is all that is required. There is no need to try to fix anything. Your contribution is your willingness, nothing more.

Prayer is a way to acknowledge the presence of Holy Spirit as a guide and friend. Prayer is equal with desire since we always get what we desire in our hearts and minds. You can think of prayer as your practice of direct connection to your higher power. It doesn't matter the method, the technique, what words you use, or how you pray. What matters is that you stay open to an experience of inner connection. Surrender in honest communication and sincerity, while earnestly acknowledging that which is felt deeply in your heart. The Holy Spirit is the healer.

True Knowledge Is Not Knowing Anything About the World

When you live in a state of nonjudgment, you naturally live in a state of ultimate freedom and compassion because you accept everyone and everything regardless of what happens. To not know anything about the world of form and to be in a state of not-knowing, opens an experience of the present moment. The I-don't-know mind is the highest state of mind, higher than "yes" or "no." This is essential.

This state of mind doesn't judge. It doesn't interpret: good, bad, right, wrong. It is close to true knowledge, the knowledge of God. Anything that you think you already know ends up being a block to true knowing. Anything you have a preconception of would block true knowing. This is because opinions and preconceptions keep you from an experience of innocent perception. You also miss both the present moment and the guidance that's available when you are occupied with intellectually "knowing" something or living in autopilot mode. In believing that you know best and that your knowledge is valuable, you identify as the opinions that you hold. Your identity becomes a small self. All personal interpretations of absolutely everything in *all* of time and space and history are wrong minded and erroneous. To hold an opinion is the same as not knowing who you are and not knowing who God is.

Now you can relax as you are looking to unlearn the habit of personal judgment and interpretation. It's a relief to know that you don't have to carry any judgment or opinion about your identity as a person— good or bad, spiritual or unspiritual, and so on. You also don't have to interpret, judge, or even understand the world, although you can choose how you perceive it, and this we will get more into later in the book. In fact, the only way to come back to divine innocence is when you can say, "Wow! I have been mistaken about absolutely everything. Not 99.9 percent mistaken. I have been completely hoodwinked; I have been completely deceived. I've been mistaken about everything!"

This is why you shouldn't struggle with the giving up of judgment, because the only awareness that you can come to is that you never, ever have been capable of it in the first place. You're truly not capable of any judgments. That's the good news!

CHAPTER 2

PERCEPTION

There's never anything inherently wrong about what's going on in the world or the way things are unfolding. Whenever you are having a problem at work, with a relationship, or anything, you are experiencing a perceptual problem. The way you are seeing it is the problem. Blaming the external world, and this includes yourself, is the ego keeping the illusion of duality going. When you get angry, it is because the ego says, "Blame this person, or blame that thing." You can blame your boss, blame the government, blame your mother, blame your past, or blame the dog. This is a world in which blame seems to be everywhere—and is seen as justified. The mind uses blame to avoid looking at the belief in separation. It blames anything that feels disagreeable to it without taking responsibility for the split and without accepting the Holy Spirit's healing of the split. But once you see that the anger comes from your own attack thoughts and grievances, always with the fearful belief of separation underneath, you can release those thoughts.

Instead of trying to define the problem as a specific situation, the first thing to do is remind yourself that it is a perceptual problem. Whether it is "I can't pay my bills," "My boyfriend said he would leave me if I don't do this," "It's been raining for four days straight, and I'm going out of my mind waiting for some sun," or "The national debt is ticking higher every day," you just say, "I have a perceptual problem." Poverty may be spreading and spreading: "I have a perceptual problem." I need the rent money in two days, and I don't know where I'm going to get it: "I have a perceptual problem."

Perception is the realm of the five senses. Perceptual problems are never real problems, although they can point us back to the one problem of believing in separation. Perception is the realm that we appear to be in. This was highlighted for me when my sister got married. The day after the wedding, people from different generations were gathered watching TV. It was a comedy special. Because there were so many of them, I couldn't see the TV. All I could see were faces turning red, eyes shifting around, some embarrassment, some downright humiliation, and some outright anger and rage. And then my brother-in-law fell out of his chair and rolled on the floor laughing.

They were all watching the same images, and they were all listening to the same sound. Yet, they were each seeing something different. They were having such diverse reactions, and they were giving their own meaning to those sounds and images. It wasn't the images that were making them laugh and making them rage. It was the beliefs in their minds that they reacted to.

We have it all backward when we think things like *You hurt my feelings,* and *If you hadn't done what you did, I wouldn't be so hurt.* So, you could say that these perceptions in the mind are associations from the past—memories and beliefs. Lesson 2 of *A Course in Miracles* teaches that you have given everything you see all the meaning that it has for you. That's all that is happening. Nothing else is ever happening. Our mind is full of past thoughts, and these past thoughts are projecting onto the world.

Caught in the Projection

The world perceived through the body's eyes and heard through the body's ears is a screen of images. It is just the shadowy reflection of the attack thoughts in the sleeping mind.

Let's use the analogy of a movie projector to explore this. Inside the projector is a glowing, brilliant, radiant light—a great metaphor for the Holy Spirit. This brilliant light seems to pass through the film, which is filled with a lot of dark images. These dark images are like attack thoughts or ego thoughts. As these thoughts are projected, what seems to be produced on the screen are shadows. To the sleeping mind, these shadows appear to have meaning. However, the only meaning the movie has is given to it by the mind—a mind that has forgotten that what it sees is just a movie. It has identified with figures on the screen and thought of itself as part of the screen, as a person among other persons. The mind then appears to be caught in the projection, identifying itself as a body.

Therefore, we need to bring the darkness—the shadowy thoughts and beliefs that are playing out on the screen of consciousness—back to the radiant light within, for this is how they will disappear. This is a way of facing what is coming up from our unconscious mind. We tend to try to avoid a lot of our problems by pushing away what is in our mind. We are trying to insulate ourselves from our problems and what lies beneath the surface of our conscious mind. The human condition is often all about trying to live a certain way or building up "the good, successful life" to protect something. This something we are trying to protect is actually a separate self-identity. The ego is terrified of any of our routines being broken because of this protectionism of the self-concept. It wants to keep the status quo so we can remain in the dream, in the projection, and not wake up. When we are asleep in the dream, we can't help but believe in what we are perceiving. That is why the Holy Spirit supports a very gentle awakening.

A world is going on in our minds: the world of images and the thoughts we're thinking. This is the basis for how we perceive the external world. The external world and the internal world are the same. They are identical. It doesn't matter if somebody is yelling or screaming at us at work, whether we're just at home thinking about when somebody was yelling and screaming, or even if we're not in touch with what the thoughts are. We just know we're feeling yucky and depressed. I call these past thoughts—thoughts that weren't created by God. They are in there, and the mind has anchored to them; it could be fear, envy, jealousy, boredom, or irritation.

Knowing this, we can see that we need to clear our perception because there is no objective world of events, circumstances, and images separate from our perception and interpretation. The realization is "My thoughts are images that I have made." What you perceive is just a motion picture of what you believe and of your thoughts.

So, when you have ego beliefs and harsh attack thoughts, you will perceive a world of fragmentation. You will perceive victimization. You can't help it. Traditional science and biology have taught us that the human being is an autonomous creature: the world is outside of this creature, and it is experienced through sight, sound, touch, smell, and taste. When light goes in through the retina, the image gets turned over in the brain, and then there are brain impulses. But we've got it all backward. It's more accurate to think of the eyes as projectors rather than receptors. The eyes are projecting what the mind is thinking and believing. Because of the filter of consciousness or ego, we sense a world that is projected through this filter, and therefore we are just drawing forth witnesses to what we believe and think all the time. We perceive only that which we believe, and so without attack thoughts in our mind, we cannot see a world of attack. That's why the only solution is in the mind.

The Levels of Mind

I once asked the Holy Spirit for a map of the mind so I could know what was going on underneath perception. I said, "It's getting a little ethereal here, give me a picture." I was shown the image below of the mind and its layers.

Think of the mind as five concentric circles. The inner areas determine the outer, and altogether, these layers compose our perceptual experience of the world, our own personal reality. The ego wants you to think that cause is at the level of perception, the outer layer. This way the ego would have you think that events are causative. In truth, this is reversed. The cause is in the center, where desire is, and the effect is on the outer ring. Everything follows from the desire of our heart.

1. *Perception* is how you see and interact with the world and includes even *what* you perceive in the world. It includes everything that the five senses report back to you.

2. *Emotions* determine your perceptions. They can be fear-based, such as guilt, shame, envy, worry, and so forth, or love-based, such as peace, joy, happiness, freedom, and so forth.

3. *Thoughts* determine your emotions. They are the ceaseless, moment-by-moment train of ideas and images passing through your mind. They can be Spirit-inspired or ego-driven.

4. *Beliefs* are the foundation of your thinking. Beliefs are concepts. Examples can be about job roles and career identity or family identity as father, mother, husband, wife, sister, brother, daughter, or son. They can be about roles of friendship, or cultural, religious, or class roles. They include opinions about the planet, society, psychology, philosophy, and politics, and beliefs about food, health, and education. As well, time and space are also actually only beliefs. All beliefs are ego-based except for one—forgiveness.

5. *Desire* is in the center and determines your beliefs. It is all about what you seek in the core of your being. You can always only choose between love or fear, Spirit or ego. With the belief in

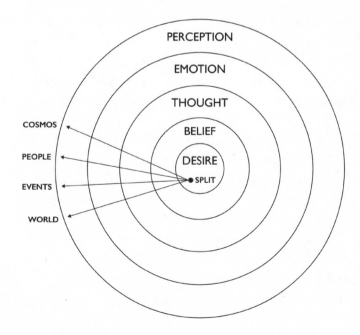

separation, desire became split. Split desire is egoic, while the single desire for love is unified and is the desire for Spirit.

When our core desire is split in impossible attempts to reconcile Spirit and ego, purity is lost. The desire in the core of our mind and being dictates our experiences on the surface of consciousness. Nothing comes to us unbidden. From a split desire, all the other layers follow. The belief becomes egoic, the thoughts are attack thoughts, the emotion is fear, and the perception becomes fragmented and distorted. Fragmented perception includes everything that we see, hear, and touch, all the different facets of the cosmos, including the people, the events, and the world of separate objects. This explains why all the differences of the entire cosmos spring from the desire for something more than the unified oneness God gives, as if we could get more than everything. But the power to change our perception rests in the core of our mind. Because of our powerful mind, the prayer or desire of our heart is always answered. This is something we will explore in depth in the following chapters.

Shifting of Our Core Desire

When we change our minds to be Spirit-inspired rather than ego-driven, our core desire has changed. It is singular rather than split. This change permeates all the layers of the mind. This is the miracle that leads to the following transformation: the belief is forgiveness, the thoughts are "real thoughts," the emotion is love, and the perception is peaceful, true perception. With the help of the miracle, the mind is turned right side up, away from its former upside-down way of being and operating.

Enlightenment or healing is a matter of desire. This is a world of distraction, isolation, and hiding from the light. If the prayer of your heart is to experience the love and the light, then the symbols or the means for this can be given or drawn to you quite rapidly.

The only problem in the world is the one in the mind. A clear understanding of the layers in the mind helps us become aware of the story— what's causing our perception as we trace back all our projections to the core desire. In doing so, we can uncover beliefs and assumptions that we may not have realized were there. The mind will continue to invest faith in these beliefs until it becomes clear that they don't offer what we truly want. When we are willing to question what we believe, with the Holy Spirit, the results are nothing less than miraculous. All that is required is a little bit of willingness to begin to see things differently. To expose and let go of old, unhelpful conditioning, we need to go into the mind step by step through all the layers.

Perception and the Movie Projector Metaphor

As we look around, we perceive the gross perceptual world. With sky, clouds, mountains, houses, bodies, trees, and grass, the gross perceptual world is the "farthest out" from the core, the farthest away from the point where we are connected to Source or God. Metaphysically, the perceptual realm is the projection of our state of mind. One of the deepest teachings I can offer you is that you cannot change the projected world; you can only change your mind (about the world). To illustrate this, let's return to the analogy of a movie projector and movie screen.

Have you ever gone to a movie when there was a glitch in the film? You know that you cannot fix the glitch by trying to fix the screen. When you try to change things that appear to be external to your own mind or look to the world for things to change, it is like going up and banging on the movie screen believing it will change the movie. What you need to do instead is check out the projector room, which, in this analogy, represents what you desire in your core.

The external world runs like the film going through the projector creating overlays. Once you are able to overlook dark thoughts (the film), the world you see lights up. But when you interpret things as painful, for example war and conflict, it is the ego's lens that you are looking through, and that is what is twisted. It is not about anything "out there" in and of itself.

Before a movie starts, there is just a beautiful, pure white light reflected on the screen. You can imagine drawing a body on it; now, we have form overlays. Then the ego names this body as male or female and puts some skin color on it. Then we can put age in there. Concepts that come from judgment and interpretation have gotten between the light source and the screen. And there we have all the problems: sexism, racism, ageism, and so on. It seems as if those are big problems in the world; we hear about them on the news, but it all stems from having a split desire in the mind.

When we can see that all is projected, all the specifics, all the differences, and also all the preferences, it is clear that what we are now really going for is an unlearning or a subtraction process. We can think of it as a process of cleaning the film. As we take steps to face and undo what's blocking us from the joy that is our birthright, we finally arrive in the miracle, in the light.

The way to come from split to unified desire is to see that the problem is not out there, outside of our minds; we have to look inside. To illustrate this, let's use the levels of mind map and insert all the seeming problems of the world on the outer layer of the mind, perception: floods, tsunamis, hurricanes, typhoons, or tornadoes; diseases like cancer, heart disease, or HIV; financial problems, economic conditions around the world, poverty, and world hunger; terrorism; and wars. We can fill in with anything we conceive of in our mind that we've been conditioned to think of as a problem within time and space on any scale or of any magnitude. It's all out there on the screen. There seems to be a myriad of external causes and external effects on the screen, but, gently, the Holy Spirit keeps singing this song to the mind: "That's not the reason why. The problem's not out there; you have to look inside." The Holy Spirit is not only telling us to look inside, but has also given us the steps, the *how* to move through illusion and to find the solution. The correction to this erroneous thought system can only happen in the mind. With Spirit's help, we can find the correction in our own minds, just like Jesus did. He simply accepted the correction for every false belief. And now Spirit is giving us a detailed roadmap. The way is made clear!

Going Back to the Projector

How do we get to a peaceful perception of the world? By not judging. The less you judge anything in your life, the more it seems like you are just watching a movie or theater play (sometimes with lots of good acting going on!). Rather than being within the movie as a character among other characters, you have the greater perspective of an observer. It's only the ego that tries to separate out and thinks it knows the motivations of all the characters, why they did certain things, and what they were thinking. The ego is constantly reading meaning into everything. And whenever you see through fragmented perception and try to analyze the characters, including your own, it gets very complicated. In fact, it's so complicated that you couldn't possibly see it as just a dance of form. You can't even enjoy the movie of life because there's too much judgment going on. And part of that judgment is control. The mind that has fallen asleep, has forgotten its Creator, and is trying to control absolutely everything. It's always showing up with an agenda. It needs to back off the screen and make its way back to the projector room.

Through the miracle, you can experience that everything is thought. It all can merge and meld into holistic perception and awareness. When that happens, it's so peaceful; there are no parts to conflict and no parts to defend and attack. Your perception becomes more and more unified in the joy. Therefore, things that others identify as problems and may even apologize for, you don't even notice; they are not in your awareness. This is how it goes with perception. It's subjective. And it is through facing your beliefs, allowing your emotions to come up, and becoming more aware of your thoughts, you will find that your perceptions become lighter. You are moving toward unified perception where your experience is more and more one of peace and harmony.

A Different Tool for Awakening to Joy

I am a huge fan of using movies as helpful tools on the journey. I see movies as modern-day parables, and the journey can be quite fun. I encourage you to explore your perception in every movie-watching experience. A spiritual journey need not be cumbersome or tiring.

Movies are an excellent way to watch your mind, to pay attention to your emotions, and to help you discover what your unconscious beliefs are. When you react emotionally to a movie, it's the same dynamic as when you react to people in your life. If you have issues with people, it's a projection of your mind. And it's the same if you have reactions to a movie—it's coming from a projection of your mind. Watching movies is an enjoyable way to wake up and heal, compared to being in a difficult family situation or in a confrontational relationship. Watching movies for healing can help you get clear in those difficult situations faster. Being aware of your state of mind, thoughts, and reactions while watching movies accelerates healing. It can be intense at first when you start to get in touch with emotions and beliefs, but it gives way to joy, and you open up more to lasting peace, happiness, and contentment. Ultimately, movies can help guide you to enlightenment.

The Spirit showed me techniques for watching movies in a new way—not as entertainment or escapism, but as a way to allow intense emotions to arise for healing. Movies can trigger memories that have been repressed and denied. When these intense emotions come up for you, pause the film so you can be present with whatever is arising for healing in the moment. Welcome the feelings so they can be released and open up to a new perspective.

EXERCISE: Enjoy the Show!

Watch the Disney movie, *The Kid*. Even if you've seen this movie before, it is guaranteed that with this new purpose, you will have a deeply meaningful and healing experience. Remember that the purpose of watching the movie is for healing the mind by releasing unconscious beliefs. Hold this intention of using it for healing clearly in your mind before you start the movie. A simple prayer can be helpful: "Holy Spirit, I invite a new and healing experience, watching this movie with You." During the movie, watch your emotions and anything that the scenarios or characters bring up for you. Even if you experience discomfort, try not to distract away from it. More than anything, be willing to stop the movie and feel and observe your emotions during intense scenes, attractive scenarios, or moments when you want to know or think you know what will happen next. Give yourself permission to stop investigating and just be with what is arising in awareness.

Following your viewing of the movie, answer these questions in your journal (you may use some of these questions for any movie that you watch going forward):

1. Do you see how observing your different perceptions allows you to identify certain emotions and maybe even beliefs? Write down the emotions and beliefs you identify.

2. Did you experience any triggers or upsets from seeing any particular scenes or conversations in the movie? What were they?

3. What were your general feelings and associations about Russ as a character in the beginning of the movie?

4. Russ seems to have a lot of stress over keeping his self-image. How might this relate to you? Do you attempt to keep a good self-image in different situations?

5. How did you feel when little Rusty confronted him about the way his life ended up as a forty-year-old—that he had no dog or girlfriend and that he does not fly planes?

6. Does this movie remind you of anything about your past that you try to hide or might still be upset about? Write down anything that feels unresolved.

7. There is a funny scene when Russ makes an attempt to find safety in a sandwich. Are there situations when you feel that your self-image begins to fail? What are the forms of "safety" that you try to use to cover insecurities?

8. How does Russ's attachment to his false identity block him from true love and happiness?

9. What enables Russ to let go of his false identity and step into an experience of love?

Release and Rest: Take some quiet time to detach and let emotions and ideas from the processing of the movie drop away. Open your mind to the Holy Spirit to wash away any remaining feelings and relax into peace. Take your time; there is never any rush.

Peace in Spiritual Perception

The power of desire is the determiner of your state of mind. You are now in the early stage of changing your perception, which really means changing your life toward the real experience of peace. Small steps can lead to some big shifts in your awareness. It's important to be vigilant with your perception and the tendency to perceive upsetting things as real problems. This is a process of looking honestly at your mind while allowing your heart's desire to be purified.

The spiritual journey will culminate when you open up to spiritual vision, the vision of Christ, which takes you beyond the body entirely, back into an awakened state. Spiritual vision is a vast experience. The observer and the observed are one through healed, peaceful perception. When you perceive the entire cosmos as unified and as neutral, you have reached true perception. It's like a happy movie that includes everything and everyone. That's how you return to your Christ awareness. You return first to this full and complete awareness that everything is really one, everything is the same, there are no differences. The purpose is to see everything through the Holy Spirit's peaceful perspective or interpretation. Therefore, "it is from your peace of mind that a peaceful perception of the world arises." In this perception, nothing is a struggle!

"The miracle is a lesson in total perception."

CHAPTER 3

FEAR

What if we knew that all the things that we do—all the plans, all the busyness, as well as drama, bewilderment, despair, and conflict—are chosen by a mind that is afraid of being present? This fear of being present is disguised as many other fears. It can be fear of being alone, fear of losing someone, fear of what other people think, fear of accidents and catastrophes, or fear of threats, violence, and abuse, to mention a few.

Fear serves one egoic purpose: to keep us from feeling the wonderment, the beauty, and the eternal calmness of the present moment. The separate mind is untrained and unwilling to keep attentive to the present since it is afraid of it. It is afraid of the Holy Spirit. The reason for this may not be apparent. It believes the ego, and thus separation from God, is real. It is attached to a tiny, imposter concept of self that is not true or real. We have all felt fear; it is a universal experience. It is an experience that exists in our minds but nevertheless, because of projection, it always seems to have external causes and also solutions, yet those solutions are never permanent. Fear locks us down. It closes us up and isolates us from the world. Until questioned, it binds us in a small and separate existence. Fear stems from a belief in a world of duality. Once fear is questioned, it will no longer rule our minds, as my friend Jenny learned through her experiences.

Jenny's Example

I was brought up in a family that went to an ecumenical church. There was a deep belief in sin and guilt. For me, what sin was always seemed strange, vague, and unclear. The teaching was that we are all sinners. As a result, I had to really face the fear of going to hell. One day, I sat on a stool in my room feeling bewildered, scared, and extremely determined all at the same time. The feeling was, "I have to follow my heart, and I have to leave my church." And the belief in hell, which to that day had been in the back of my mind, surfaced. The fear that I could possibly go to hell was in the forefront. But I responded with, "Okay, if I go to hell, I will still do this; I still want to follow my heart. I have to." And looking back at it now, I know that the fear itself is what hell is.

Facing this fear shook me to the core, and I could only sit through it, allowing the fear to move through. Yes, potentially I would actually go to hell by this move, and if so, it would be worth it; it would be my choice. I faced the deepest depression of my life. I was in a dark tunnel, and one day I was at the end of it, facing the back with no exit. There was nothing else rising in front of me; it was like being stuck in the darkest part of a deep cave. A friend, whom I trusted, called me that day. She asked if I wanted to share how I was doing. I spoke about the darkness, and after the call, I realized I had turned around and was facing the way out of the tunnel. From then on, I could feel the possibility of light and healing and I began to take steps toward the light.

Stepping out of Normal

On the spiritual journey, you will probably find that you will feel called to make some changes in your life, like Jenny did. But because of fear, you may find many reasons not to make a move or even take a step. Even if you have some hesitation at first, when you feel ready, you will find that it's worth it to feel uncomfortable, to let go of your routines in order to find all the joy of God's love that's available. It can feel like a solo journey at times because you have to go within to find the answers. At other times, companions show up to help you along the way.

When I was in graduate school, I would take long walks in the woods. During these walks, I'd ask myself, "What am I doing this for? Is there a purpose for studying at university?" And the ego would rattle off, "Yes, you need to have a degree because you need to have a good job. Because if you want to have a relationship, you can't be broke. This is why you are here, and this is why you have been here for ten years. Just keep at it, and we'll get through this phase." All of my reasons for being there were fearful, based on my fear of consequences.

Becoming aware of this poor motivation for my life got me in touch with a deep desire to open up to the guidance of Holy Spirit. I would ask, "Why am I here? Am I afraid of something? Is there something driving me to get all this education? Is there something pushing me from underneath? Am I afraid of something besides what the world would call a 'fully engaged life?'" The more I took the questions inward, the more Jesus was able to show me that it was freedom, peace, happiness, joy, love, and intimacy that I wanted. He showed me that I had many beliefs about what one has to do in this world to get those things. And it was those beliefs that were driving me. He said: "If you listen to Me, I will show you how to experience the things you want, through Me. In other words, through listening and then following Me, it will come from the inside of your mind. It won't come from any event or outcome in the world."

This turned me in the right direction. In the beginning, I was astounded to see what a huge percentage of my actions were motivated by the fear of consequences. It could have been tempting to judge myself at that point, but I was determined not to do that. I was happy to discover how plugged in to the fear of consequences I was. I was happy to begin to unplug with Jesus and the Holy Spirit's help. I found that to be very practical. It was something I could contemplate and ponder. I knew it was going to be a big job. I knew I wasn't going to take a pill and wake up the next day free of fear. I knew it would take contemplation and mind training. But I had A Course in Miracles, and it was a great tool to burrow deep into the mind.

As I mentioned in the introduction, the mind can be directed by one of two thought systems: either of fear or of love. The ego-thought system produces fear. The Holy Spirit's thought system produces love. The ego speaks first because it is impulsive. It is usually very harsh and critical. And the voice of the Spirit has to wait patiently, and then, when your mind is open, you can experience how He is there, unceasingly and very gently reminding you of the truth of who you are. The ego wants you to believe in its thought system and tricks to keep you asleep and dreaming, while the Spirit wants you to see your thoughts, your feelings, and your beliefs so you can become aware of them and start to loosen the bindings that limit you. To know this simplifies things as you realize you can choose which thought system to use. It is a decision in the mind.

You will see that you are making decisions all along the way. You're vacillating between two thought systems and between two emotions, and there's got to be a way to bring an end to it. You can make a choice. It is a matter of being alert to which voice you will give your attention. Whichever you give more attention to is the one that will become stronger in awareness. It's very much like the old saying about the black and the white wolves in the mind: one represents fear, and the other represents love. The question is: Which wolf will you feed?

The Ring of Fear

In the explanation of the levels of mind in chapter 2, we saw that underneath the gross perceptual world is a layer of emotion. A *Course in Miracles* calls this "the ring of fear." This whole world—everything that we perceive through the five senses—is built on unconscious fear. How can this be? How does our fear translate into objects of time and space: houses, buildings, streets, and people? By the power of our mind. The mind simply can only see what it believes, which is why we need to release false beliefs. In the end, the spiritual journey becomes all about facing this unconscious fear. This is the transformation of the projected world into peace.

When we take steps inward on the way to discover peace and true freedom, we first encounter the ring of fear, and it usually gets quite intense. In addition to fear, all of our other emotions are right underneath the far outer ring of perception as well. This means we really need to get in touch with our emotions as a starting point. If we ever want to reach the point of truth deep within our minds, we need to engage the natural process of allowing our emotions. The ego tries to control us by scaring us with many hypothetical consequences, so we push down and suppress all our emotions.

Most of us weren't raised to get in touch with our emotions and thoughts. Many of us, if we were feeling upset, angry, or belligerent, were told, "Go to your room!" or "You're grounded!" The response wasn't "Oh sweetie, tell me what you are thinking." Your parents were probably not Christlike psychotherapists filled with unconditional love and positive regard. They probably didn't say, "Let's get in touch with those thoughts underneath the fact that you just punched a hole in the wall." They said, "You are grounded! You will fix that hole in your wall, and we're taking away your allowance." We were usually met with a lot of harshness when our emotions came up.

There is a different way of relating with feelings, and when you understand the metaphysics of the mind, you discover what's beyond your perception down in the levels of mind. You can become much more sensitive to what's underneath the surface. Sometimes in meditation if you start to sink very deeply inward, a very surprising fear can come up, and it will seem to come from nowhere. You are getting in touch with the darkness of the unconscious mind. This is fear that's buried very deep. It is the reason why a personal identity was made. The personal identity was made to cover a very deep fear that you could be separate from God, from everything, from your Self—that you could be alienated from your Father and from oneness and be utterly lost. Mystics and saints have often shared that they encounter this fear when they begin letting go of their personal identity and they are coming closer to a merge with God. The stillness inside is so powerful that it can seem to burn up the "self." This is a huge threat to the ego, which is why it feels like a burning up or dissolving.

The fear-based ego-belief system is based on having no safety in a dark world of hurts and needs, and of believing in the reality of victims and victimizers. This is so only because of an identification in the mind with the self as the body. But how could we truly know of safety and comfort except to identify with something real and true, something that cannot die or change?

Everyone who is asleep and dreaming in this world is actually afraid of the Holy Spirit. This is so because even though people's lives are not happy and fulfilled in time, there is a familiarity to linear time. The things and activities of linear time are believed to be safe, while the Holy Spirit is associated with the unknown and is something completely different than anything in time. In the state of oneness, the mind is naturally at peace. The first fear was the fall from grace. It was a tremendous shift in mind, from loving, peaceful, and happy to terrifying and frightening. So, each step that you take with the Holy Spirit will have some reverberations of fear associated with it. Because even though you are awakening from a nightmare, the ego is afraid of this awakening. The ego is afraid that it will be annihilated, that it will cease to exist.

When we perceive something fearful, we can always allow ourselves to take a moment to pause rather than react. By taking a moment to open our minds and invite Holy Spirit into our perception, we invite a miraculous shift in how we see things, and we can start to let go of habitual reacting and conditioned behaviors. We open up to inspiration.

The beauty of the journey to happiness and freedom is that we all have the power to follow our inspiration and Spirit. We choose this and no longer live based on fear of consequences. Otherwise, how would we ever get past this fear of love? We make a decision to no longer go for the seemingly prudent, safe choice based on our past learning. We decide against the closed loop of the past and allow for the miracle, allow for the inspiration.

EXERCISE: Looking at Fear

When fear (or other negative, upsetting emotions) comes up, you can be alert to it. You can face it with a "bring it on" attitude where you're actually happy that you've got something to work with since releasing fear and doubt is really releasing the grip of a false identity. This exercise has the potential to help you to deepen in trust beyond desired results and outcomes—time-based desires and wishes that your sleeping mind hopes to attain and achieve because of the belief that they are safe and can offer something of value.

Make sure that you have half an hour to an hour to yourself. Choose a current life situation that brings up fear or maybe just some anxiety or worry. It could be around losing a job or a relationship, or it could be other fear-based issues around family or friends. Fear can also be disguised as anger because there is always fear underneath anger. Try to be aware of other defenses or self-concepts that may cover the feelings. Take a look at ideas such as "I am a person who never get worried, anxious, or fearful. I am strong and competent. Nothing ever worries me." These may be cover-ups, and you may not yet be aware of a deeper part of your mind that actually has a lot of fear or anxiety, which explains why the defense was built up in the first place.

Keep this particular fearful life situation in awareness and relax for a moment. You are now going to look inward, following these steps.

1. In your journal, write down all your feelings and thoughts about the situation.

2. Is there a certain meaning and importance you have given to this situation? How are you perceiving the situation? How does it affect your peace of mind? Close your eyes if it helps you focus.

3. Now take a moment and inquire on this very important question: *Where do I believe my safety lies?* Sit with this question for a moment. Write down the thoughts that come to mind. Make sure you don't censor yourself or come up with an answer that you believe is "right." Allow yourself to experience these thoughts as they reflect the beliefs that you hold around safety. Then write down all your associations to this fear until you feel complete.

4. Slowly read this list of possible fears:

   • fear of not having enough money

   • fear of not being a good enough father, mother, son, brother, or sister

- fear that I actually feel some misery inside and that it will get worse

- fear of my own anger or someone else's anger

- fear of standing up for myself

- fear of being tiny, small, and unimportant

- fear that I don't really know enough

- fear of expressing myself, especially the love

- fear of making a dramatic change in my relationship

- fear that I might not "make it"

- fear of losing special attention from others

- fear of sexual intimacy

- fear of touching others or being touched

- fear of connecting and communicating with others

- fear of attraction to certain people

- fear that someone will reject me

- fear of trusting

- fear of facing the day when I wake up

Do some of the items in the list relate to you? Take a moment to first notice and then journal your reactions and discomforts with these particular fears.

5. Take a few minutes to settle in and, using free association, list additional fears that come to mind. Allow all your thoughts and emotions around these fears to pour out in your journal.

6. You are now going to relax and invite the Spirit to shift your perception. Gently and prayerfully go over each fear and say: "Holy Spirit, I hand this fear about _____ over

to you." Feel free to add, "Be you in charge." Take enough time to allow yourself to feel the release for each one. Continue on with this handover until you feel a calm and assuring restfulness. You may feel that the fears are loosened from your mind or even gone!

Fears Can Become Possibilities

Fear in the mind is nothing other than the ego actively attacking your peace of mind. This means that you often experience a lot of attack thoughts and doubt thoughts. In those moments, it's important to be able to face the fears and really ask, "What am I afraid of?" When you are able to see your fears and what's behind them, you can really get into the strength of choosing to be with the Spirit and realizing there's nothing that can threaten you at all. The fear does leave. I live a completely fearless life because I allowed all the darkness to come up. I stopped hiding and protecting it. I don't use any kind of defense mechanisms. When you refuse to stuff it down and let it fully come up, it comes, and you go back to the light in the present now.

This is important in any situation where you want to know your heart's calling and your way back to peace. You need to be very honest with yourself and look at what you're afraid to lose. When what you are afraid of is seen, you will be in a space to tell the Holy Spirit, "Just show me if it is Your will." Your mind is now open to all possibilities and all options. Then, from a place of feeling the joy and the peace, you can easily access deeper inspiration. And you will be able to see a lot of signs and symbols because the Holy Spirit doesn't just provide guidance; He always provides the means to achieve it too!

I join you in accepting the next steps in this journey. I encourage you to follow your heart in the face of any fears that you may experience. Our journey together is one of inspiration—of opening to all that is possible with the Holy Spirit.

CHAPTER 4

GUILT

There will be times when you feel resistance to the Holy Spirit, when the ego says, "Stop! No! Stay away from my life." Or it will say, "I will give you some parts of my life, but I'm going to keep some to myself." As we listen to and follow the Holy Spirit, we become more and more willing to give over all of our pictures, the whole film, to Him.

Let's zoom in on one of fear's major derivatives: guilt. We all know how it feels to have feelings of guilt and shame. Most of the time, we associate feelings of guilt and shame with something in form, something we think we have done wrong, or something that we didn't do that was expected of us, and we feel like we came up short. This shows us that guilt always seems to be related to behavior, whether it's our behavior or somebody else's behavior.

By refusing to face the guilt of separation, we project this guilt, which I call "ontological" guilt, onto many different things. We can feel guilty about food. We can feel guilty about sexuality, body image, or past memories of behaviors. I have met people who have been in prison for what the world would judge very shameful crimes. I have met people who would look me in the eye and feel me out: "Can I expose a secret to you? And will you still love me afterward?" Once they know that yes, I will, then they tell me that they have killed somebody. Or they reveal their deepest darkest secret, their hidden secret of what they find most shameful, what they believe makes them a sinner, makes them unloving, unlovable, and so forth. When someone exposes their guilt this way, I stay with the presence of love and don't judge whatever they did. And in their exposing it, it is automatically handed over to the Holy Spirit. Their first step of unveiling the ontological guilt has been taken.

The ego wields guilt. That is why you reinforce a feeling of guilt anytime you use the body or the world for the ego's purposes. The ego's purpose could be possessiveness or "getting." It can be to defend, attack, compete, or use the body for pride or pleasure. The guilt is not inherent in anything. It's only the purpose we give to things that determines whether we feel guilt or peace. The purpose we give to anything can either reinforce the separation or it can be used for healing and forgiveness. Let's take the example of food. Food is generally a huge target for the projection of a lot of guilt. The truth is that deep-down, people don't feel guilty around fatty or sugary foods, even though the nutritionists tell us not to eat these foods. Even brands play on our guilt by marketing products as "guilty pleasures," "guiltily delicious," and "sinfully delicious." But there aren't good foods and bad foods. There isn't anything wrong with ice creams or cookies, sweets or meats. We should not feel guilty about eating certain foods. The belief in guilt is in the mind. There is no guilt in the foods, nor can eating them cause any guilt at all, although it sometimes seems to get projected that way. Like with anything else, we can open up to Spirit's guidance around what to eat.

It is the Holy Spirit's task to purify the mind. You need to let Him reinterpret everything that the ego made, including the body. This is not something that you can try to skip over; there is going to be a lot of guilt that will come up as you relate in this world. Along the spiritual journey, the ego defense mechanisms attempt to minimize fear and guilt without actually letting them go. Instead, the ego minimizes the fear and guilt to the point of being tolerable—so that you will keep them! The ego-thought system does not want to get rid of them, so it acts ingeniously: minimize the intensity to keep you trapped. It is as if you were forced to agree to drink a cup of lethal poison but were granted one wish of deciding how you would drink it. Your wish was to mix the poison with the ocean first, let it blend in, and then you fill your cup. That is what the ego is doing; it lets you dilute the poison before you drink it. It dilutes the guilt so it gets unrecognizable and acceptable to the sleeping mind. But diluted poison is still poison although it's harder to recognize.

The Origin of Guilt

Guilt is the feeling that something has gone wrong. The mind gets fixated on it, gripping something that is not loving, but how do you become aware of and release this feeling of wrongness?

Guilt is also associated with linear time. Projection and guilt are the "making" of time, for without those, there is only timeless eternity, where all is one. Because the ego invented linear time, it tells you that you were guilty in the past, that there has been much wrongdoing in the past, and that the present moment is nothing or insignificant. It rolls over or skips the present moment where the answer of peace is and moves into the future, making us believe that the future will be the same as the past. This guilt comes from way down inside. It originates in believing that we are separate from God. The ego-thought system uses linear time to keep the mind trapped in guilt, and then it maintains the guilt by the repetition of this same mistake of separation, over and over again. But it is all a big trick to keep you feeling you have done something wrong.

In this way, guilt has nothing to do with behaviors. Guilt gets generated from the core split in the mind (see the levels of mind discussion in chapter 2), not from things in the world, although it is immediately projected out as the world of form. This means that the experience of guilt is solely a result of the purpose the ego gives to things. Most people are not consciously aware of this, so no matter how much we try to change behavior, guilt is still there. The belief in hell, the devil, or some dark force separates the mind from the experience of being one with God. Metaphysically, it is our own guilt that projects the whole idea of an external dark force or hell. Since the ego believes in opposites and is scared of God and love, it makes up ideas such as hell, the devil, and sin. It is as if the ego is using what should be the most sacred to scare the mind with opposite ideas. For example, Christianity in its core is pure. It is supposed to lead people into God. Jesus's pure teachings—present in mystical Christianity, Gnosticism, and *The Urantia Book IV*—are all about that. And the ego seems to take what is the purest and make it dark to scare people. This separation guilt is all unconscious. Most people don't come home from an emotionally bad day and tell their partner, "Dammit, it's that belief I've separated from God; I've been acting it out all day." We don't get into traffic and say: "That guy tried to cut me off! Ah…separation from God again!" And then we don't eat lunch and say, "Oh, I overate; I feel bloated…ahhh…separation from God." This separation from God arises, and we feel so guilty. But we don't go through the day consciously thinking that we have separated from God. We are not aware that this separation is our only problem, nor are we asking ourselves why we keep playing this game. We are not aware that it's ontological guilt that's causing all the specific problems.

In attempting to fix our life or to heal, we mistakenly focus very strongly on specifics. The mind gets tangled and complicated; that's why we can work with a psychotherapist for years and make very little headway—because we focus on the wrong thing. It is like rearranging the deck chairs on the *Titanic* while the ship is going down. As long as we have guilt coming up, there is a deep fear of love way down in the mind. Whether we're aware of it or not, there is a tremendous terror of love. Of course, it's the ego's terror, and as long as we're identified with the ego, we'll feel its emotions. We'll feel the ego's guilt.

How Ego Wields Guilt to Keep Us Trapped

We need to disidentify from the ego, to expose it, and show its nothing-ness. Once we are disidentified from the ego, we are free of guilt forever. *So how is the ego maintaining guilt?* What are its tricks at the bottom of the mind where the guilt actually occurs?

There is *a lot* of guilt in the mind. The ego has it wired that way for a reason: to keep us trapped in a small self-concept that is very limited and experientially very far from our true Self. The way it does this is through memories, conditioning, and anticipation. We just keep having certain memories and experiencing events that reinforce the guilt over and over again. This is because guilt is wired to behaviors. But no matter how much we try to behave and be a good little boy or girl and no matter how old we get, because of the guilt, we still seem to mess up. And we still seem to have behaviors that we associate with guilt. It seems like we are caught with our leg in a trap, and we can't get out of it because the guilt just recirculates and recycles through the memories and the conditioning. And our anticipation that this is just the way it is keeps projecting the guilt out onto the future, and so we keep experiencing it.

There is a line in *A Course in Miracles* that says, "For you must learn that guilt is always totally insane, and has no reason." That is a pretty clear teaching from Jesus: there is no reason for guilt. Another line says, "All anger is nothing more than an attempt to make someone feel guilty." I call this the unholy trinity: guilt, fear, and anger. They are coming from the ego belief system in an attempt to project. It's a dynamic where, if you get angry enough, somebody is supposed to admit guilt or feel bad. It's all an egoic attempt to not look at our own guilt, which actually only maintains our guilt and anger. My great suggestion is that when you have those emotions arising, do not buy in to ego justifications or rationalizations for them or look for causes in the world to blame. You can never fully know the bigger picture of mind while the ego is believed to be real.

We can only feel angry, guilty, or afraid while we still have the belief of separation active in our mind. All guilt arises from the attempt to think apart from how God thinks. God is love and the illusion of guilt can only come from having thoughts that aren't of God. They must be ego thoughts because that's the belief in separation from God. *A Course in Miracles* states that guilt feelings are just a sign that we don't know that God Himself orders our thoughts and that we believe we can think apart from Him.

How does this relate to all the problems we see in the world? To believe you can think apart from God is "the authority problem." It's believing you can author yourself. So, the authority problem is a question of authorship: Am I the author of me, or is God the author of me? Am I as God created me, as Spirit, or can I make myself something other than Spirit: flesh, separate, tiny, and little? It happens in the mind, but it gets projected to form. It plays out when children have problems with parents. Think about two-year-old children and the first "No!" coming toward Mom or Dad. You know how it goes when the teen years come, parents get authoritative: "You are drinking; we're going to give you a curfew;

we're taking away your driving privileges." The war may start against parents and transfer to classmates and teachers, and then, as the young adult grows up, there are authority issues with police officers, politicians, lawyers, and bosses. It goes on and on. It's all a projection of the initial authority issue, of thinking we are the author of our self.

Guilt and judgment always go together. We judge because we feel guilty. But where does the guilt come from? Where does that deep onto-logical feeling of wrongness, of separation, come from? Not the personal guilt of I, personally, am unworthy or I'm not good enough, which most people deal with for their entire lifespan. I mean that fundamental feeling of wrongness, that something has gone dramatically wrong, that all this fragmentation wasn't meant to be—the core guilt. It comes from the belief that you can order your own thoughts, that you can judge. It's misusing the power of your mind. It's like saying, "Hey, I'm in time and space now, and I can do any damn well thing I want to do here. I've got my currency to spend. I've got my time to spend." Giving this power to ego is almost like giving a small child a credit card and saying, "Go at it! Go have some fun with that credit card and do whatever you want with it. I don't care!" Ego believes this time is yours, it's a currency to spend between birth and death, and you can do whatever you want. And, wow! Look at the variety that's involved with that, if you consider all the years, the centuries that this has been going on, and all the different ways an individual life is spent: as a Roman centurion, as a prostitute, as a gover-nor, as an athlete, as an office worker or doctor, as a husband or wife, as a nurse or carpenter or whatever. There are all kinds of combinations. It's almost like the new age teaching you might have seen: "Create your own reality." That's what's underneath this: the belief that you've got a menu in time and space, and you can pick and choose and select from all the different possibilities, all the images, and make a conglomerate, a synthetic personal self.

With a sense of these dynamics that go on in the mind, you can learn, not to stop judging, but to let the Holy Spirit judge for you. The Holy Spirit, Who knows us as we truly are, judges everyone and every-thing as innocent. We can refer to the Biblical expression: judge not, lest you be judged. That was spoken by Jesus two thousand years ago. Do you know anyone who has been able to completely follow these words?

Returning Home to Our Father

Jesus told the parable of the prodigal son, where one son left after asking for his inheritance. Off he went and used his entire inheritance for riotous living until he had nothing, until he was hungry, until his only job was feeding the pigs and he was eating the husks. And after some time, he said, "Even my father's servants have more than me. Maybe I should go back." And he went back in shame; he went back in guilt. He went back with his head bowed low.

But before he even got close to home, his father came running down the road, running to welcome, running to celebrate. In the same way, our shame, guilt, and believed wrongdoings are met with open arms. The father can only see the son's innocence, so he celebrates with a party, by killing a fatted calf. And then the other son, the dutiful son, the son that tried to play it safe and do all the right things, sees the condemned brother come back. He says, "What is happening here? A party? I have stayed here dutifully by your side all along and not once have you killed a calf for me. This wanderer, this betrayer, this weak one who blew it all, you welcome him back and have a party?" The dutiful one is angry. And the father says to him, "Dear son, all that I have is yours; it has always been yours. But your brother, my son, he was lost, and now he is found." There is nothing more important than to be found, to find our true inheritance again, regardless of what seemed to happen when we were lost.

This second chance is the olive branch that is there for all of us. God is saying, "Just take the olive branch, just take the branch of peace." This realization is what the second coming of the Christ means. It's our Self-realization. When the awareness of our true Self dawns—the knowledge that all is forgiven and that we are one in God where we have always been—we know that we are nothing but mind. This mind is whole and complete. It never dreamed of fear, loss, and separation. It is free and happy in God. It is guiltless—innocent!

EXERCISE: Looking at Guilt—
From Blame to Innocence

To listen to a recorded version of this exercise, go to http://www.
newharbinger.com/41870. (There are a host of other materials available for download there. See the very back of this book for more information.)

Sometimes we really want to be right about a situation. Whenever the pain of guilt or the desire to be right arises, remember that if you yield to it, you are deciding against your happiness, and you will not learn how to be happy.

In this two-part exercise, you are going use a situation to look closely at your experiences of blame and guilt and move toward the release of them. Acknowledge and invite the presence of Spirit, your higher power, to guide your mind through this process.

Part 1: Exploring the Feelings of Blame and Guilt

Identify a person you blame for hurting you. In your journal, answer the following questions:

1. What do you blame this person for?

2. Why do you think they are guilty?

3. How are you maintaining the story that they are guilty in your mind?

4. In this situation, what do you think you did that you regret or feel guilty about?

Prayer for Release from Guilt

I ask you for help, Holy Spirit, to see myself and my friend as you created us.

I cannot do this alone, so I ask that You be with me now.

I want to be happy. Holy Spirit, help me to decide for peace.

I give this situation or relationship over to You. I trust that You will guide me in the way ahead.

Peace of mind is a present decision, which I gratefully choose right now!

Blame and guilt only seemed possible because I was determined to hold on to a false belief about who I am and who my friend is.

I let go of the meaning I gave to the situation and open my mind to the present—absolved and innocent.

I am grateful for the realization that the cause of my upset, which I thought was in the world, was actually only an unquestioned belief and decision in my mind.

I have decided anew for my peace of mind.

Part 2: Innocence

Stay with the same person and situation. You and they have a shared identity in God as perfect innocence. Spend a moment and reflect on this. When you're ready, answer the following questions in your journal:

1. Do you feel this person deserves to be innocent? Why or why not?

2. If you cannot see that you are both innocent, can you feel a sense of wanting to be right?

3. If being right means that you will be unhappy, do you still want to be right?

4. Can you see how accepting your innocence releases both of you from guilt?

5. What is innocence to you? Write it down and focus your attention on how this experience of innocence feels to you.

> **6.** Take a moment now and reflect on this prayer:
>
> *I am the work of God, and His work is wholly lovable and wholly loving. This is how a man must think of himself in his heart because this is what he is.*

To further process and deepen your healing experience using the levels of mind, you can find a downloadable worksheet at http://www.newharbinger.com/41870.

Let Miracles Replace Guilt Thoughts

Nothing we perceive is there by accident; it is just exactly as it is because that is the way our mind wants it to be. By making our unconscious guilt conscious and then releasing it, we can heal and start to perceive the world differently. We have a choice in how to interpret things. In truth, there is no guilt going on at all. It has no purpose. Only as long as we still have some unconscious desire for guilt do we interpret the world in a harsh way. We can learn to be more gentle with ourselves and free ourselves from those harsh interpretations and be light-hearted! We can laugh and sing in joy and really feel that we are moving on in the right direction. Why not let every day be like that?

In our hearts, we can find the innocence even when things seem to fall apart and when things seem to implode. Don't try to hold it together! We are going Home. We are waking up. There is no need to make it any more complicated than that. We are here to expose the ego's guilt game. Everything the ego does—every scheme, every defense, every trick in the book—is aimed at perpetuating guilt. Let it arise and release it.

You need to realize how closely you are identified with the thoughts you think. If you project judgments onto the world, how could you not feel guilty? Of course, in truth, you are not guilty because God didn't create guilt. God didn't create a stream of guilt thoughts and say, "This is my beloved stream of guilt thoughts, in whom I am well pleased!" God doesn't work that way! No, He says, "This is my beloved son, in whom I am well pleased." God is pleased with the Christ, the Christ of pure love, pure innocence, which is you, and not a stream of guilt thoughts!

Where the ego's purpose is to make you guilty, Spirit's purpose is to extend innocence. That is why you need to go inward and bring the guilt to the Holy Spirit. Bring that darkness to the light so you see that the guilt has nothing at all to do with the world or your behaviors. As you go deeper, you start to realize that there is never a reason to feel guilty—it is just part of that false ego belief system. You start to become aware that the way out is miracles. The more miraculous your life becomes, the more habitually miracle-minded you become, and you experience the innocence that comes from miracle-mindedness.

You have had glimmers of this innocence. You don't need to change. You don't need to become better at something. You don't need to fix something. You are just perfect. In the next chapter, we will bring more clarity to this as we get into the importance of our thoughts and the power of our minds.

Think of all your relationships. How would it feel if you saw everybody as perfect? What if when somebody came to you and said, "Oh, I feel so bad for what I've done," and you could just smile and give them a big hug and say, "I love you so much." When you can give that gift to yourself, you have the power to give that gift to everyone: to all of your friends, family members, coworkers, and people in the grocery store. And it feels so good to give that gift. It must come from the Holy Spirit because the ego could never conceive of such a gift. It has been the greatest joy in my life to give the gift of innocence away: "You are not guilty; you are innocent. I see you as innocent, I will treat you as innocent, and I will think of you as innocent." It is only by giving away that which you want for yourself that you can escape from guilt!

CHAPTER 5

PRIVATE THOUGHTS

We communicate through words, through language, and by sharing our thoughts. This happens every day: in our families, in our schools, and at work. When we share our thoughts with others, we expand our view, connect, and grow. Communication can also be wordless and still be shared clearly, for example through body language. But if we don't have someone to talk to, we believe that our thoughts are not shared. It seems like we can think about whatever we want, and nobody else knows about it. This is the belief that we have privacy inside our minds. But our thoughts alone make up the whole (seemingly private) world we see.

At our *Course in Miracles*–inspired monastery, we have no vows of poverty, chastity, or obedience as they do in traditional monasteries. Instead, we have a guideline: we encourage everyone to have no private thoughts and to expose what has been hidden.

Private minds with private thoughts seem to be the very basis of the human condition: humans value privacy, autonomy, and independence. It is said that these things make the human being, but it is a game of pretense, a ruse. These unreal concepts and ideas generate a fiction of the human race, a fiction of individuality and separateness. In this fiction, it seems each person goes their own way and leads a distinct life apart, only to meet with others at certain times. This has never brought us consistent joy, happiness, peace, or contentment. Stemming from the belief in separation, private minds and private thoughts have us wandering, lost in time and space. We just need to open up and share. Returning to Jenny's story, she says:

In my early twenties, my marriage was not happy. It felt abusive, and my husband even raged a lot. I didn't feel like I had anyone to talk to about it. Then I met a pastor at a conference who I found very, very trustworthy. I poured out my whole heart to him, all my experiences, and all the pain from my marriage. This pastor just listened to me. He was very open-minded, very interested, engaged, and patient, and I felt such an opening in my heart and in my mind. It felt so valuable, like a long-sought lifeline. I felt seen and heard. This opened me to the many steps I needed to take to move forward and heal. Opening up my private thoughts opened up my life.

The urge to keep stuff within and not share comes from our urge to defend and protect ourselves. But the need to be defensive can only come when we have identified with an illusion of our self. If you take a thought that comes, a feeling of mild concern, or a bit of worry, and follow it down into your mind, you will find an image of yourself that is not the real you. It is a picture that was made to take the place of your true Self.

It's not that good or bad things happen to us. We can learn to not judge the form and instead see that everything is an opportunity to expose our fears, doubts, and beliefs. We've been accustomed to taking things on, to taking things personally, to feeling bad, and to feeling like we're not worthy of sharing, not worthy of *being*.

Experiencing and perceiving an external world is rooted in hiding and holding on to private thoughts. When you become more aware of your thoughts and beliefs, you'll find that what seems to be happening in form is connected to your inner feeling experience. The internal and the external world aren't really different; they merge. It seems like there's a world outside the mind, but it's actually not out there. It's synonymous with mind. This means you really don't have interpersonal relationship problems. You really don't have any physical problems. You really don't have issues with what could happen to the environment. It's all in your mind. It's all mental.

The Core Private Thought

When it comes to healing the mind and opening up to freedom and joy, the big shift happens when we open up our most private thoughts. Underneath all the others, there is one core secret that is intolerable to hold in mind, and it is this idea: "I am separate from God." This core private thought marks the birth of a belief in time and projects a whole world. This thought puts everything fearful "out there" as well as what is believed to be enjoyable. This is where beliefs such as pleasure and pain come in attempting to strengthen the idea that you are a body. We can say that thoughts of valuing the body and identification with it are diluted private thoughts that cover the core private thought of separation. Essentially, all the thoughts that separate a "me" and a "you" are private thoughts.

Thoughts that lead you away from an experience of this present moment, or any thoughts involving time, are private thoughts. This is because time, as used by the ego, excludes the experience of the present, the miracle. A private thought always involves the past or the future in one way or another. Regret of something that seems to have happened in the past or worry about something that can happen in a hypothetical future are examples of this. These thoughts, often concerns, worries, or even hopes, only involve the perception of a separate individual. They are therefore also called hypothetical thoughts. Hypothetically speaking, as-if, in the future, something may or may not occur. If you really watch your thoughts as they roll through, you'll see that there are a lot of hypothetical, private thoughts. Some of them are judged to be very desirable, which explains why you think about them over and over. Some of them are very fearful or worrisome and have a lot of doubts, anger, and guilt attached to them. But they are all part of a mechanism to distract you and keep you from experiencing the present moment.

The Holy Spirit knows that the sleeping mind is heavily invested in private thoughts. When the Self is realized and there is an experience of pure oneness, there are no longer any experiences of private thoughts, yet the condition of being in this world is to believe in those thoughts. In fact, they are believed to be the only reality. So in truth, I have no private thoughts, but as a separate self, all that I am aware of is private thoughts. This must mean that the separate self is not who I am. By their very nature, private thoughts come from an individual mind, with memories and thoughts of the past as well as future planning and looking forward to things. So, through exposing all your thoughts to the Holy Spirit and maybe to a very trusted friend, you are opening up to a completely different experience, different than you've ever had before.

You have surely noticed that there are a lot of emotions connected to private thoughts, and that's why it can seem like the human condition is just an emotional rollercoaster ride. Up and down. People will even say, "Life is meant to be a series of challenges," and "It's inevitable that you will have challenges every day." And this is an experience most people have, which is based solely on these private thoughts and the emotions that come with them. If we had to give a definition of God's will for us, it would be perfect happiness. God's will is definitely not for a rollercoaster ride of emotions and painful experiences. That is why it seems to take a lot of conscious willingness to allow private thoughts to come into awareness and then to be willing to *not* protect them, *not* push them down or repress them, and *not* to deny them. Just allow them to come into awareness, then let them go, and give them to the Holy Spirit.

This is not like a lot of spiritualities where we were taught to accentuate the positives and eliminate the negatives, or to use positive affirmations. That's a common thing that people talk about on the spiritual path, as if you can just eliminate the negative and then have only positive thoughts in your mind. But the positive thoughts and the negative thoughts are both coming from a dualistic perspective, a part of a continuum, and it's the very continuum that's the block.

So, the attainment of happiness and inner peace is a matter of willingness to *not* hide and protect private thoughts. Because we judge our private thoughts as terrible or wrong, we hide them. There's a mask that the mind wears. It has the personality mask on with underlying beliefs and thoughts that it's too afraid to face and expose because they are believed to be real. We believe that if people knew about these thoughts, then they wouldn't want to be around us.

But as we expose these private thoughts more and more, we come to a point where we say, "A*aah*, these are just thoughts in my mind. I can't believe I held onto them for so long." The only way to reach the real you, or to reach that sense of invulnerability and a constant state of being happy, is to let go of the mask, the part of you that plays a role as a personality self. Let go of the belief that those thoughts are really who you are and question the validity of those thoughts. The ego set it up that way to obscure the truth about who you are. "And yet it is only the hidden that can terrify, not for what it is, but for its hiddenness." Ego made up all the differences that led to all the private thoughts. Therefore, it's only through the awareness that there are no private minds that we know freedom and love as it really is, the love that is at the core of our being, the love that is our true, divine self.

Open Up, Share, and Be Free

We only hide our thoughts out of fear and guilt, and this is just a holding on to a make-believe identity of guilt. When we truly give private thoughts to the Holy Spirit, we let them go forever. It's like talking to your best friend. The best friend does not take these thoughts seriously and may laugh when you share them, and then you laugh too because you see how silly they are. This is how healing occurs.

We have heard and often felt the deep value of communication. The holy instant is the experience of total communication. It is what I call communion. Communion with God is total communication in which everything is out in the open. The whole journey to enlightenment and self-actualization is about voluntarily, willingly, and gently letting the private thoughts come up into your awareness. Seeing that they no longer serve you, you realize that you don't need them for survival. You don't need them for a sense of well-being. You will relax, sink into the present moment, and experience that everything you could ever want or ever need is in this very moment.

It takes a lot of trust to let go of thoughts that you believe bring about safety, security, and many, many desirable things. But they haven't truly brought about safety. It's been more like a wheel; you've just kept thinking about them over and over. The wheel does not bring peace of mind. This wheel, a wheel of distraction, is what has kept you apart from the present moment in experience. When you go deeper, you start to get insights about how your everyday life can only reflect what's in your mind—your thoughts. I call them the "top forty"—the thoughts that recur over and over. Work with your top forty; they are topics and opportunities that are just waiting to be dissolved. Try to not interfere with the healing that's always occurring.

Some of my best times, the times that I have enjoyed the most on Earth, are when I have done long retreats, and people line up for one-on-one sessions. This often happens after profound talks since people get in touch with a strong desire to open up and share what's in their heart. Some people unload their deepest darkest secrets, their deepest shames, or their deepest fear. I honor this deeply. It is immensely sincere and beautiful. I love being used as an instrument of innocence and healing. Often when I sit with someone, their eyes are saying, "Can I trust you? Will you still love me after I speak these next words to you?" And then they go for it. What follows these sessions is usually a moment of sparkly eyes, and we are both in happiness and love because the love of God transcends anything that the ego can come up with, any memory, any perception. We have an experience of our divine innocence, which is what we all want.

A very helpful step toward not taking the world so seriously and not taking things personally is to have a safe environment, a safe atmosphere like a best friend with whom you can release your private thoughts and grievances. Imagine having the presence and spaciousness, to have someone, maybe your spouse, a coworker, a close friend, or a relative that you can just pour your heart out to, knowing that they love you. You trust them, and you know that they are not going to take anything you say personally; you can let up all the darkest things. I think that was the original intention behind the confessional booth of the Catholic Church—unburdening yourself. Talking to someone who is loving and caring is a symbol of giving it over to God and not holding on to anything. The more you say, "I want to heal; I want to bring this up, to release it, and to give it over," the more you hear others speaking the exact same thoughts and sharing the exact same feelings. And when you are the one listening to them, you think, *Oh, how could she think that about herself? How could he believe that? I feel love for him; she is beautiful.* And the feeling is *I love you,* once the private thoughts are expressed!

Whether you are giving thoughts over or hearing someone else express private thoughts, you see clearly that it is the ego being exposed, and that it is not who you or they are. You can truly see these thoughts, and they get lighter and lighter and funnier and funnier. What is really powerful is that we do not try to fix the thoughts or adjust the story. We are just letting them go so a deeper awareness can come and take the place of the busy thoughts. Issues simply dissolve, and you get to see that the Holy Spirit is really the healer. It is practicing the prayer of bringing illusions to the truth and praying to bring the darkness to the light of love that brings the healing!

EXERCISE: Express Those Private Thoughts

Do this exercise when you can spend an hour by yourself. Get your journal, and silence your cell phone. This is a time set aside just for you.

Part 1: Write a Letter

Imagine someone whom you can trust completely, whom you could say absolutely anything to and they will not pass judgment on you. This person can be real or imagined; you could even write to the Holy Spirit. This friend listens to you lovingly and is not affected by anything you say or by any of the thoughts that you are ashamed of. This is someone who listens to you with a caring heart and offers you unconditional love.

You are now going to write a letter to this friend. Sit quietly and allow all private thoughts to come to your mind. Write down your thoughts in this letter: thoughts you have hidden, thoughts that cause fear, thoughts of judgment on yourself, thoughts that you think would cause others to judge you, thoughts you feel ashamed of, unloving thoughts you have toward others or yourself, thoughts you worry would cause a person to extract their love from you.

Recall the importance of bringing private thoughts up to be exposed: when anything is hidden, it cannot be healed. Take some deep breaths, and continue to write all hidden thoughts and thoughts that are so intolerable that you have avoided writing them down. Exposing these thoughts is where the healing lies. They can now be offered up. This letter is proof that you are willing to look at absolutely anything that comes up on your journey to healing.

Once you have finished writing, sit or stand in front of a mirror and read your letter aloud. Allow yourself to feel the emotions that surface, knowing that a loving presence exists that accepts you unconditionally regardless of these thoughts.

The next steps are up to you. You can keep this letter, share it with a trusted friend, or if you feel like a symbolic act of letting these old thoughts go, you can even burn it. These thoughts have no effect on your worth. What matters is that you allowed your private thoughts to surface, acknowledged them, and then released them.

Take plenty of time to nurture yourself and rest after this exercise. Let any remaining emotions, thoughts, or self-judgments pass; let them not hinder the peace that is your birthright. If you were able to fully give yourself to this exercise, you will feel a deeper acceptance of yourself and appreciation of the healing you are experiencing.

Part 2: Venturing into the Open

Slowly go through the following questions one at a time. In your journal, prayerfully write down your thoughts and responses without reading ahead to the next question.

1. Choose an intimate relationship or a friendship where you notice that you hold back from expressing your thoughts and feelings.

2. Inquire about why you think you hold back from expressing your thoughts in this relationship.

3. How do you feel when you are holding back? How do you react?

4. What are you afraid will happen if you are authentic and transparent with your thoughts?

5. How would your life be different if you allowed yourself to express what you are thinking and feeling to those closest to you?

In the Light of Love, Communication Washes Ego Away

Once you have exposed everything, the Spirit in you will want to extend, but the ego is afraid of that, so it may be another obstacle to overcome. The ego will want you to hold back, to keep your love, your joy, and your happiness bottled up. Allow yourself to share, to just let it pour out so you can start to realize that you don't need to be afraid of that love. Love pours through us, expresses through us, like a cleansing, washing, purifying experience, and it's only the ego that gets terrified. Keep in awareness that the ego knows that if love keeps pouring out, then it will be washed away. The ego wants to exist, so for it, hiding becomes a matter of survival.

Choosing ego through keeping private thoughts is often an unconscious decision. It is the belief that you can harbor thoughts that you would not share and that your safety lies in keeping thoughts to yourself alone. For with private thoughts, you share only what *you* would decide to share. This shuts off the potential for full communication with those around you and with God, who surrounds all of you together. Every thought you keep hidden shuts communication off. So, continue to open up to sharing and extending love, and the ego obstacles and fear will fall away.

As long as you give in to ego's preference to have private thoughts and keep them, you cannot experience the holy instant. The holy instant happens in the present moment without the ego thoughts of the past and the future. The holy instant is a time in which you receive and give perfect communication. It is a moment in time when your mind is open both to receive and give. The holy instant is the acceptance of the single will that governs all thought. This is how you come to experience the miracles that you have been unconscious of. In the sacred and holy experience of this moment, the mind seeks to change nothing, but merely to accept everything. This holy instant, this moment, is the recognition that all minds are in communication.

PART II

MIRACLES WITHIN

CHAPTER 6

FINDING TRUE GUIDANCE

Have you ever heard about athletes who get "in the zone"? How they can get into a state while exercising or during a match that is completely intuitive and inner directed, which allows them to respond with perfect grace to the external world? In that moment, they are not thinking about reaching a goal but are fully aligned with and rested in the present. We can get in a similar "holy zone" by opening to being guided.

As humans, we focus a lot on "doing" rather than "being": What am I going to do today? What do I do next? What are you going to do? Is what you are going to do going to jive with what I am going to do? None of these questions are truly helpful since they're not directed to the Holy Spirit nor open for guidance. They lead to a scattered experience of our day where nothing seems to really make sense. Things seem to happen without a clear feeling of purpose behind them. It is a common problem to, out of habit, decide what to do before we ask for guidance. It is a habit of a mind that believes it is a human being—a mind that believes it is a "doer." We should call it a human "doing" instead of a human being. Peace of mind can only come when we have reversed this habit of deciding first what to do and then asking for guidance. We have to get into the habit of truly asking Holy Spirit what He would have us do and say. Being open to ask for guidance undoes the independence and autonomy of separation and opens us up to a healthy experience of God-dependency.

Being in a childlike state of not knowing is one of the most important steps toward learning to hear the inner voice of Spirit and beginning to live a life without fear. Children are such wonderful examples in their great trust. Young children walking with their parents are amazing to watch because they put their hand up and ask to be led. Their minds are open and receptive to discover and learn because they trust that they are safely led and shown the way. A first step toward this state of "I don't know" and being guided is opening your mind and being willing to loosen your definitions about what everything means. The goal is to be so inner-directed by this voice that you no longer take any of your "cues" from the external world unless you recognize them as Spirit within. My friend Jenny shares:

> I felt as if my mind and my life were like a maze that I couldn't make sense of, and where else could I go other than toward God? I felt like I had to have clarity from Spirit or God because I couldn't rely on myself. I felt like I didn't have the big picture and therefore couldn't decide what was best in every situation. I needed a capital H help. True help. I realized that this world had no answers and no guidance to give me.

Learning to hear and follow guidance, I went through a lot of cleansing and clearing, a lot of tears for many years, and a lot of praying, discernment lessons, and asking. Sometimes I would just ask and ask, and I would hear this gentle wisdom inside me. It would say: "It is good that you are starting to ask Me for guidance, but don't become obsessive. There is no need to ask for every single decision during a day." Should I take my shoes off? Should I go out the door? Don't become obsessive with it. Just trust in the Holy Spirit. Feel an opening to the guidance and trust that you are going to do just great, that Spirit has got it. The Holy Spirit is saying: "I will direct you; just be willing to come in My direction, and you will see that it is going to get easier and easier for you. It will be more like a flow when you start to align your mind with Me."

Many years ago, I sensed that I needed and wanted better discernment between the ego and the Holy Spirit. I asked the Holy Spirit for guidance.

Me: Can You give me something practical that can help me? Even if it's going to take time, I'm willing to work on it.

Holy Spirit: Look at your life and start to consider how many of your everyday actions are based on a fear of consequences. Take for instance your job. Would you go to that job every day unless you had a fear of consequences?

Me: Of course not. I would not be going to work every day if I had no fear of consequences, if I didn't want some idea of security for my future.

Holy Spirit: This fear blocks a sense of being guided. Now go through all the nuances that seem to be part of each day, including the very subtle aspects, such as not wanting to let people down, not wanting to hurt people's feelings, and not wanting to step on anyone's toes. See what else is based on the fear of consequences.

I started to do that with my life, to pay attention as I went through my days. Something profound started to happen because I realized that the opposite of fearing consequences is to be motivated by love. Imagine if you were motivated only by love and nothing else. Imagine how different it would be if there was no sense of fear pushing you. How would your life go? You'd start to investigate what you do things for. Being motivated by love helps you discern ego guidance from God's guidance.

When I started following love, I was amazed at the practicality and ease that came with starting to hear this true guidance. If we need a word of cheer or comfort, it is there. If we need specific instruction, it is there. If we believe we need anything, that voice, that one voice, is always the practical answer. And for me, that's where the simplicity came in. I found out that tuning into my inner voice, tuning into the Holy Spirit, was really the only goal worth having. Life became very simple in that. Trying to listen to the ego is where the complexity seems to come in. But once you understand how the ego works, you can lay it aside!

Turning Away from Ego Guidance

The ego is very ingenious. It even wants to come along on the spiritual path. The ego can make you a polished spiritual self-concept. It can take over any concept just to preserve itself. It can be very sneaky. To get in touch with whether you are following the Holy Spirit or ego, you need to discern how you truly feel. If you're feeling happy, light, and peaceful, that's when the guidance is coming. If you try to listen to and follow guidance and don't feel joy, you may have a discernment lesson going on because the Holy Spirit always inspires a true sense of joy.

A classic example of the sneakiness of the ego is when it starts saying things like, "I kind of like this guidance thing. I can do anything I'm pleased doing, and I'll just call it guidance." Take a domestic situation when you live with someone as an example. One party says: "If you don't take the garbage out..." and the other party says: "I was not guided to take the garbage out." And the first one says: "I'm not guided to take the garbage out either." You've got to watch this ego; it's very clever: "Well, my holy spirit told me..." "Well, actually, my holy spirit told me...." You can tell that you're listening to the ego when you start using the word "my." This is the ego trying to use the idea of guidance for its own purposes.

The ego does not want you to have anything to do with guidance unless it is its own guidance—and it wants you to be a slave to it. The ego likes that, but it is offended by the Holy Spirit's guidance. It wants to protect itself since the Spirit's guidance will undo it. Therefore, it wants you to be dependent on it for everything. It does not want you to realize that the mind is causative and that nothing can happen that the mind has not asked for, that nothing comes from the "outside." When you realize that nothing is external and that there are no external causes or effects, the game is over for the ego. You have effectively ended its tyranny, this false rulership, and you have accepted the strength and power exactly as it is, in mind and as mind.

One of the deep truths that isn't really known in the world is that if you have a wrong-minded perception, a misguided behavior will always follow. This is because thoughts and images of forms are one and the same. If you have wrong-minded thoughts, you will inevitably be mis-guided. Actions and behaviors are not autonomous or separate from your thoughts and beliefs. What you do comes from what you think. Without exception, this is so. What you do is determined by your perception of a situation. There is great relief in knowing that what you do comes only from what you think and believe and that there is nothing outside of your mind. This is why you need guidance from a wisdom beyond your own thoughts and belief system. You can relax and ease your way into this alignment with the guidance of the Holy Spirit within.

The difficulty is not really in finding out which voice is the Holy Spirit's and which one is the ego's. When you have fear in the mind, the ego will actively attack the Holy Spirit's guidance. So, there could be a lot of attack thoughts or doubt thoughts coming up with certain guid-ance. Therefore, rather than asking whether it's Spirit or ego, an impor-tant step is to question what you are afraid of when you want to know the guidance in a specific situation. And you can decide to be very honest with yourself and look at what you're afraid to lose. When what you're afraid to lose is not hidden, your mind is open to all possibilities and all options. You will be in a space to tell the Holy Spirit, "Just show me if it is Your will." Then you can feel the joy and peace that comes with feeling the Holy Spirit's guidance. You will be able to see a lot of signs and symbols. Symbols and metaphors of harmony and union align the mind with the Holy Spirit.

When you open your mind to guidance, you can see that guidance always offers a very obvious and easy option. The question of whether it comes from the ego or the Spirit becomes unnecessary after you have faced your specific fears. True guidance is always from the Spirit, and the ego is only providing fears and doubts that you need to heal and clear, but never true guidance.

Merging into a Glorious Flow

The experience of listening for true guidance is like being in a constant state of prayer. All of a sudden, you feel how natural this is, and you understand that you will need to make no decisions by yourself. You will let Spirit decide for you. Be You in charge, Spirit! You know the way. You know the way out of the dream of separation. There is a shift happening when you surrender to Spirit this way. You come from an autonomous separate sense of self in a world apart and merge into a glorious flow that has always been your natural state. It is absolutely delightful to move into a day with an open mind that does not have a to-do list and is not set on outcomes—being wide open to let the day be like a blank canvas that can be painted with all the beautiful splashing colors. How free and how wonderful! "What is going to happen today? Oh, a splash of green, some red, some yellow." You can sit and behold the painting as it appears right before you and really be in the glory of it, without trying to control it, without trying to be the artist. Just be the witness Self, the observer. It is delightful.

Following guidance is a pathway to this ultimate experience. You come without preconceptions, you come without ideas of outcomes, but you come with a willingness to be shown, to receive that which is given, and to trust that everything is for your awakening. That is what carries you higher and higher to this ultimate experience.

Spirituality must be practical. This is why it comes down to really opening up to guidance day to day, to letting Holy Spirit go before you and lead you in the decisions of your life. You are making decisions to unwind from the ego-thought system. The only way you authentically unwind is to decide with God, to decide with Spirit, as you move forward. It is beautiful and very, very practical. It can almost become like the song of your heart: "Today I will make no decisions by myself. Instead, I want to be led. I am ready to be led." As you get into the joy of joining, it becomes obvious that this is truly the way because there is lightness and happiness with it.

We can get to an experience of this gentle presence and guidance together with others. If two individuals are deeply attuned to each other and to the Holy Spirit, they can actually hear the same guidance simultaneously. This is a glorious experience. It's like becoming one with another being. This is an experience apart from time, a holy instant when you see no difference between yourself and the other. In that moment, there are no bodies or persons. It is a true moment of being one mind. You can experience great harmony when you have synchronicities like this. You look into each other's eyes and say: "Are you hearing what I'm hearing?" "Mmm mmm…" You don't even have to finish a sentence because you are both feeling the intuitive yes.

EXERCISE: Opening to Spirit's Guidance

To listen to a recorded version of this exercise, go to http://www .newharbinger.com/41870.

Before you begin this exercise, take a few breaths and relax your mind. Close your eyes and take as much time as you need to feel present and focused. As you move through this assignment, I encourage you to allow any reactions or emotions to come up freely. Don't restrict or censor yourself.

Think of an area in your life where you feel you need some direction right now, big or small. Close your eyes and relax into a space where you feel attentive, clear, and calm. Bring the area to mind and hold it in awareness as you prepare to offer it to the Holy Spirit. Allow any images to appear in your mind that represent the essence of this issue for you. Take your time. Now, imagine a large round golden platter in front of you, and see yourself placing your issue on this golden platter and offering it to Spirit. Think of Spirit as a vast, warm light. Then let it go. Don't think about it. Try not to think of anything at all. You have brought your issue to the Spirit; now relax!

Imagine giving yourself over to the Holy Spirit completely in this moment. Stay in this place of communion with the Holy Spirit for as long as it feels helpful. Just be in the moment without expectation. Now, exercise your willingness and present capacity to trust. If you find yourself reverting back to worrying about the situation and taking it back into your mind, that's okay. Relax and forgive yourself, and just begin again by placing the issue on the platter and offering it to Spirit. And let it go! Take your time. Know that whether you get a specific answer or not now, you can feel calm and reassured because you have handed it over to Spirit. He will guide you. Drop any desire for a particular outcome but remain alert—and expect miracles!

A Prayer for Guidance

I open my heart to You, Holy Spirit.

I am willing to ask You to guide my every step and to follow You,

For I know this is my way Home.

Help me to be in a consistent state of peace,

to let go of all my resistance, my fears, and

the conflicting wishes that stop me

from knowing Your peace and guidance.

Amen.

As you come out of the meditation and prayer, try to stay with this sense of calm and connection and know that divine guidance has you. Allow yourself to be open as to what to do next. Be alert to feeling or hearing from within an answer or a direction to take. It can come from external signs or symbols, through what someone says, or just as a feeling from within. There can be a yes or a no if this applies. Watch out for any tendency to use the ego intellect. Instead, allow your intuition (Holy Spirit) to lead you. No matter what the guidance is, trust that it *will* be what makes you happy—if you follow it. For God's will for you *is* happiness.

Sweet Humility

It is the response to the inner question, How do I feel?, along with the commitment to follow the voice of the Holy Spirit, that ultimately will make it possible to discern between the two opposite thought systems. The more you heal and become present, the more you will be able to identify how the ego's direction is always based on fear, while the Holy Spirit's direction always comes with peace, like an all-embracing divine wave of love.

You may now start to realize that if you open your heart up to this ultimate experience, what you really want and need is true humbleness, the humbleness of beginning to see that "I do not know." When you think you already know, you will never ask for guidance. This is why being in the I-don't-know state of mind is so powerful when it comes to learning to hear and follow the inner voice of God. Allowing yourself to not know is relaxing, and this is where you can begin to practice your trust, something that we will explore and go deeply into in the next chapter.

When you move toward a life of guidance, you become like a child who easily lays their old toys aside for a much more fulfilling and all-inclusive purpose. Following guidance leads to peace. It leads to everything that is best for the whole universe. With any decision that flows very easily, you can trust that Holy Spirit is guiding. You are meant to have an easy life. It's the ego that wants to give you challenges and make things complicated and difficult. The ease and simplicity of the Spirit are always available, and you can feel them when you are in a humble state of willingness to follow. With practice, trusting and following inner guidance becomes very natural.

CHAPTER 7

TRUST

Trust is the primary characteristic we need to cultivate when we start our spiritual journey. Then other characteristics will follow, such as honesty, gentleness, and joy. They all rest on trust. This is why trust in the Holy Spirit is very important.

A singer-songwriter friend in Nashville, Tennessee was not finding any more singing jobs. The doors were closing. I shared with her that sometimes we are tempted to ask ourselves or the Holy Spirit, "How can I keep my job?" even though this is presuming that we should keep our job. Are we open to widening our view? Maybe there are other prayers or other questions that we can ask, such as, "Is this the job I should keep? Is this the job You would want for me, Holy Spirit? Is me working at this job the best for the whole universe, or do You have something else for me?" This woman found out that the Holy Spirit had a whole new life to offer her, a life that would truly get her in touch with her heart's calling, and that is why she could no longer find any singing jobs. She was ready to trust her next big step in life.

The Holy Spirit's Greater Plan

It seems like when it comes to jobs, careers, relationships, and houses, we put a lot of importance on these decisions. It is as if we want to handle it all on our own. We say to the Holy Spirit, "You just help me be peaceful, and I will handle all the rest myself. I will handle the children, the job, the house, and the people." It is as if we are saying, "You give me the peace, and I will run my life." We do not realize that these goals do not go together. When we try to run some aspects of our life, we are putting our personality first and the Holy Spirit second.

Everything is constantly changing in this world. With some of the changes, we think, *Hmm...I like this,* and sometimes we think, *This is a threat, and it could be very, very dangerous or risky.* When we study or watch our mind, we can see that the sense of threat must be coming from some kind of interpretation or meaning that we give to situations. When I would have a situation where I could lose my job, I would start paying close attention to my thoughts and feelings, and I noticed that I was afraid of the outcome of losing the job. This was because of the certain meaning and importance I had given to that job. The question becomes, Can I shift my perception and come to the trust that leads to an experience of literally being sustained by the love of God?

There came a point in my journey when I realized that I had to trust that all of my needs would be met. That's when I made the decision to trust that I would be taken care of. And looking back, I see that my needs have never not been met since. It's been a beautiful journey of trust and opening in awareness, and it inspired me to write this poem.

Be gentle with yourself on this inward journey.

Accept the symbols that come to you with gladness and appreciation.

Let the Holy Spirit use the symbols to remind you of the inner beauty that is far beyond appearances.

Let the colors and the sights and smells and sounds wash through your mind as reminders of the vastness and glory of being!

Discover the beauty of the Holy Spirit's purpose.

I Surrendered to Trust and Found Joy

For me, opening to trust started with reading. I read everything from Maslow to Mother Teresa. Like most people, I was searching for a sense of purpose and meaning, and even a way of somehow understanding the human condition. I was searching in philosophy, psychology, and religion. I felt that there must be something beyond what the world and society presented. But I had no clue how to reach it. I explored and investigated. Psychologist Abraham Maslow created the helpful theory of a hierarchy of needs, which states that we need to meet our basic survival needs first, before moving on to higher order needs. Mother Teresa demonstrated the same thing. If someone is sick, hungry, or ill in some way, their most basic needs must be taken care of first. You wouldn't try to preach the gospel of Jesus Christ to a starving child. You would pick the child off the street, take him in, and then feed the child and clothe the child.

And so, in my developing of trust, reading books about these values was very helpful. I felt a tickle in my heart, a glee, and joy when I would come across ideas that really resonated and that I could really recognize as coming from God. While reading books was a very safe way of developing trust, starting to follow the Holy Spirit's guidance in daily tasks and movements brought about feelings of trepidation. Fear and doubt arose because asking where to go and whom to talk to or call was so counter to the way I had been living my life. And yet, I pushed through my fear and doubt and started following the guidance I was hearing. And it was amazing. I felt bursts of joy after I got off the phone and after I visited somebody in the hospital or paid a visit to their house. I was just swelling with joy because I listened and followed even when the ego was scared or telling me not to do it. The ego voice in my mind was saying things like: "You are going to lose your autonomy. You are going to lose your individuality if you keep following that voice." But I just kept at it. I liked that feeling of joy! I wanted more of it. I began to lose myself in that joy, and I started to discover my true Self. I found that I could trust the little prompts from the Holy Spirit in everything I did. And the more I trusted, the clearer the guidance became, and the more joyful I got.

From Survival to Divine Providence

One morning, I woke up with the Bee Gees' song "Stayin' Alive" in my mind. With it was the uncomfortable feeling that everyone is just trying to survive in this world, trying to stay alive. Think about how much energy people devote to this. It's all about survival, security, safety, and planning for the future. So much effort is put into keeping the body alive. We need to shift our consciousness from putting all that effort and energy into maintaining the body to putting that same effort and energy into forgiving our illusory thoughts, feelings, and beliefs, and remembering Spirit, our natural spiritual reality.

We need trust to shift from staying alive and going nowhere to being alive, to the joy, happiness, and vitality of our Christ being, our true Self. As we deepen in trust, we see that everything we need will be provided, without our own effort; we won't even have to think of it. This is new and big. You can treat it like an experiment but not like a test where you, for example, travel to a far-off town with no money to see if you will be provided for. It's more than that. It's saying, "Starting right now, right here in this moment, what if I decide to trust that if I'm being authentic, if I'm being transparent, and if I'm open to healing and happiness, that everything that I would need for healing and happiness will be provided?" This is the promise of oneness, of love, that everything you need to experience happiness will be provided.

A Divine Trust

What complicates life and impedes trust are the ambitions of wanting "more" or wanting something to be different. Whenever we get away from the simplicity of this moment, it gets very complicated. Any wants can start to torture us if they start looping in our minds because we are confused by thinking that these wants bring anything of value. The key is to begin to relax and to trust. And I am not talking about trusting the monetary system, trusting in governments, or even trusting a human being. I am talking about a divine trust, trusting that the Holy Spirit will offer us everything that we need to find happiness.

Here is how Jenny arrived at the importance of practicing trust.

I used to be very fearful of life in this world. I thought that there were threats around every corner and in each turn of events, threats of ending up alone and isolated. I didn't feel at home in this world, and the future was just this big unknown. Even simple things seemed to be complicated, so figuring out what I was going to do with my life felt impossible. What did I want to do and become? I didn't know, and I didn't want to make something up or just figure something out. I wanted to know that there was a purpose for it; I was extremely uncomfortable with just "getting on with life" in some job. I wanted it to be purposeful and not at random. I felt I needed to find something else, something other than the conventional way, something that I could trust would truly sustain me, my mind, my heart, and my being. It didn't seem like that was going to be anything that this world could offer. I needed to be led by Holy Spirit.

It dawned on me that this was the way to learn to trust life—by staying connected with God or the Holy Spirit. I felt that it wasn't worth doing anything without an experience of that connection. It was as if I suddenly realized that God had to do everything through me for me to know who I am and what the purpose for my life was. It was daunting, but from that moment, it has been a journey; there have been a lot of tears, doubts, and hesitations because how do you learn to open up to and always feel the presence of God in all that you do? Well, I saw no other option than to try it out, to practice trust.

Daring to Trust Paves the Way for Miracles

Faith and trust, which are synonymous, are not quantifiable. Either we trust or we don't. Either we have faith or we don't. We can't say that we have a little or a lot of trust. In order to accept the shift from our ordinary experience of life to experiencing the glory of the present moment, we need to strengthen our trust in the Divine. The divine trust we are talking about involves letting go of our attraction to a personal perspective and gradually creating the space to embrace a wholly unified perspective. To trust and live a truly devoted life, we need a step-by-step process, like children do as they grow. It takes a lot of trust for children to learn. They must trust their caregivers. This kind of trust is the key to the whole spiritual journey.

Trust depends on whose hand is guiding us. That is why we work on discernment between our true Self and the imposter self, the ego. The extent to which we give faith and trust to the imposter is the extent that we do not know our true identity. We learn to discern between the imposter and our true Self through becoming aware of how we feel. At any moment, we can ask, How do I feel? and the answer will allow us to discern where the guidance comes from. We are strengthened in our ability to discern as we practice this more and more, and as our divine trust increase, fear dissolves.

The more trusting you become, the more relaxed you become. Then when you notice a reaction or an emotion arising, you can see it is a good thing because it helps you see where the ego still has a hold on the mind. You are here to welcome what's unconscious so you can release it. You are not here to try to put on a performance. You are not even here to get things right because trying to get things right in form was part of the game to cover your feelings of unworthiness.

Developing trust in the Holy Spirit can be experienced as challenging, disconcerting, and uncomfortable. If some people knew this ahead of time, they might be afraid and look for something they think is a little more gentle. A lot of people would say, "Turn this off," or "Let's switch to another program. Let's try ballet or something a little softer." But when you go deeper, the rewards in terms of an experience are immense.

The Holy Spirit's plan is to help loosen the mind from what it thinks it needs without a feeling of sacrifice. Because the egoic interpretation of following the Holy Spirit is through the lens of loss, it is rarely experienced as gentle, but it is good to know that gentleness and lack of sacrifice is what's available.

The belief in sacrifice can play out in many different ways. Since this is a world of apparent choices, it seems that to choose one thing means that we miss out on other things. The possibility of "missing out" this way makes us feel like we are always lacking in one way or another. Developing a state of trust requires letting go of the importance of trying to choose the right form and instead seeing that the real choice is for a happy state of mind. The outcome in form is not so important, yet feeling the importance of our purpose is where our happiness lies.

Following inspiration and being guided with all the daily choices will build trust and pave the way for a miraculous state of mind. Because when you go deeper, you will see that you haven't lost anything. There is no sacrifice involved, and the rewards in terms of peace of mind are immeasurable. When you develop the ability to accept things as they come into your life, doors of happiness seem to open in front of you, one after another.

Stressors Reveal Our Level of Trust

There can be challenges in life that help us see where we are with our trust. We can use them as barometers for how much we trust when it comes down to something like the death of a loved one, the death of a pet, a break-up, a natural catastrophe, or other psychological stressors. How well do we react? Does it move us into faith, trust, and a deeper prayer? Do we grow stronger through those trials and tribulations, or do we buckle and feel crushed? Does it feel like there is no hope? These experiences can become opportunities. We can open up to allow them to spur us into a much deeper trust where we rely on Spirit much more than on circumstances.

This is a very straightforward pathway; it is really an experiential pathway. We need experiences to show us that we are on the right track and that we can continue to trust. If we took steps and we didn't feel any lightness, lightheartedness, or bursts of joy and happiness, then we might even feel suspicion, "Okay, I took that step, and…?" It needs to be an experiential journey. We need experiences to replace the past conditioning. We need some bright experiences that lead us on, like a child who is led: "Good, good, good, now come, take another step. Keep coming, keep coming!"

There came a point when Jesus said to me that I had finished my last job working for a paycheck and reciprocity. He said. "You will now be used in ways you can't even imagine. You're mine now, and I'm going to use you." That's how my life has been since 1990. During the first five years, I traveled around the United States and Canada with no home or apartment, not even a tent. I would watch the sun come up, and when evening came and I didn't have a place to sleep, I would just wait and see what would be given. There were no hotels or motels. I had an attitude of, "What is offered?" I was taken into many different homes and had many miraculous holy encounters. That was like a miraculous five-year period of "the son of man has no place to lay his head." The Holy Spirit told me to get used to it and that through trust, I would feel that He would take care of me; that He would lead me and guide me in everything that I do.

The first months of those five years were the most difficult only because I had so much pride, past learning, and conditioning, and I was thinking a lot about how I could take care of myself. Because of this, I realized I just had to be willing to take my hands off the steering wheel. When I would try to grab it back, Jesus reminded me, "Trust Me." And little by little, I started to trust in the Spirit and Jesus. Sometimes I would go to A Course in Miracles groups while traveling, not knowing where I would sleep the next night, and then three different people at the group would say, "Come and stay at my home." So, it wouldn't be a question of whether I would have a place to sleep, but about which friend I was supposed to stay with. It was like the Holy Spirit wanted to show me another angle, that I was going to be taken care of. I needed only to pay attention, and He would direct the plan moment by moment.

These experiences built up a lot of trust and also launched me into seeing that I was perfectly taken care of wherever I would go. I got to see that I didn't have to use my lifetime of past learning and ten years of full-time university. Instead, I had a lot to unlearn. Jesus said, "We have some big boulders we've got to knock off your shoulders in order for you to be truly helpful." I couldn't continue to hold onto the arrogance of thinking that I could direct my own way in this world and of believing that I knew enough to navigate time and space.

To let go into trust and let the Holy Spirit lead the way reverses the ego mentality that says that if we want to do something, we have to come up with the means. God knows the prayer of our heart before we even utter a word. We are invited to a place of silence deep inside the mind, to find an experience of purpose and intention. Purpose and intention are all about an inner connection with the Holy Spirit. It is an experience of a strength and clarity that shows the way.

Trust is the willingness to dive into presence and authentically "go for it." You come to a state of not planning anything; you follow the strong inner compass that is the Holy Spirit, moment by moment. You may not know where this is leading you, but one thing is certain, it will be miraculous!

I am sure that as children, we did not express to Mum and Dad that we didn't care or plan for ourselves. We did not want the consequences, the reactions. "What are you going to do with your day?" "Nothing!" Or better yet, "I will see how it unfolds." "What about your chores?" "I will see how they unfold." We would think those thoughts when we were children; we just would not say them. But now it is like a new day, a new start, a new heart, and a happy day filled with joy. Isn't it great? That is our theme: God's will for us is perfect happiness, and we are just like children opening up to that experience. The prayer of our heart is "Show me, show me!" This is how we trust and learn to become God-dependent. "Except ye become as little children" means that unless you fully recognize your complete dependence on God, you cannot know the real power of your true relationship with Him.

I have always loved the curiosity of children because curiosity is a reflection of openness. If you are curious, you don't think you already know. That is so important; that is one of those things you cultivate, just staying curious and open to being shown. It's very much like when you are on a trust-walk where they blindfold you, and you put your arms out and trust your guide to lead you and show you. I have done a number of those experiential trust-walks over the years, and it is just fantastic because you really have to let go of what you think you know with your senses. You are blindfolded, you have your hand out, and your guide is with you in every step. It is intuitive trust, moment by moment, that gets us to a place of deep peace and joy.

This journey with the Holy Spirit requires trust and gentleness, and by patting yourself on the back and being grateful for every little willingness that you can muster, you will naturally grow in trust and open up to miracles. When you start to live in the miracle, your concerns and struggles disappear not to come back again.

EXERCISE: Leap of Trust

Take some time now to look inward. Invite the Holy Spirit to join you in preparation for this assignment.

Reminding yourself of the miracles that you have experienced and then sharing them is a very helpful way to reinforce the truth in your mind and to build trust. Allow a time when you were guided to take a "leap of trust" to arise in your mind. It could be when you felt compelled to contact someone or had a feeling that it was time to· change jobs. In your journal, write down your responses to these questions.

1. Describe the situation when you were being called to make a decision or take action.

2. Do you recall what you feared you could lose if you took that leap? Describe any thoughts and feelings of hesitation.

3. What compelled you to take that leap of faith, even though you couldn't be sure of the outcome?

4. What was your experience afterward? How did you and everyone else in the situation benefit from your willingness to trust?

5. Are there any other steps on your horizon that you are fearing to take? Explore all your thoughts and feelings in your journal so that they may be dispelled.

In prayer and trust, know that peace and love are your desired outcomes. Let this notion support your intention to move forward with clarity!

Prayer: Spirit, Here I Am

A very short prayer that can open you up to trust is "Spirit, here I am." Say this prayer and wait quietly with an open mind. Stay attentive and relaxed. Watch what comes. Use this prayer to connect to the deep quiet experience of the Holy Spirit in your mind. Your focus is finding the quiet center within where the light in your mind can be welcomed and revealed. Let go of any sense of a need to do something. Instead, just be and witness this moment. When you are able to find the place of alert stillness in your mind, notice how it feels completely natural to trust. *Spirit, here I am.*

When you feel ready, take your pen and journal and make some notes of how this time of prayer has been for you. Then, if you're inspired to, write a poem about your current experience of trust in the Holy Spirit or maybe a prayer springs forth from your heart's desire to strengthen your level of trust.

Be still and know that trust settles every problem now!

Trusting What Is Given

When we practice trust, things coming our way will be seen as truly given gifts rather than threats or problems. We all have miracles waiting for us in the present. Miracles want to come through in a very beautiful way, but we have to allow for them. If we freeze into "should I" and "could I," then we are getting locked into the ego's doubts and comparisons, and we close ourselves off from trust.

There can surely be periods of disorientation. These come because we are loosening from the ego's hold on how we live, and its laws of scarcity, lack, defenses, and reciprocity. You're going to have a lot of reactions and reflexes coming from a fear of the light. But the good news is that from these disorientation periods, you're going to come out sailing and soaring in the most glorious state of mind that you could ever want.

At first, miracles can seem a little strange because you are not used to them. You are not used to arriving on time to a meeting that seemed impossible to make. You are not used to the Holy Spirit arranging time and space for you and life being like a wonderful flow. The ego may try to dismiss the miracles and push these experiences out of awareness, but the more you hang with it, the more consistent is the experience of peace of mind and joy.

I was guided from one job to another in a series. I was not guided to just quit all jobs because I had debts, and it doesn't work very well to quit all your jobs when you have debts. So, I was guided to work to pay off my debts. I saw that the jobs were used to help me heal certain aspects of my mind and become more dependent on the Holy Spirit. I asked to be shown which jobs I should take. Once I was at the job, it was just as important to understand what was guided, and so I would ask Holy Spirit, "How can I be most helpful here?" It was very practical, and this experience showed me that I just need to trust Him. I need nothing but this trust. Because with jobs and relationships, we cannot always judge what is most beneficial for our healing.

Sometimes people who have lost their jobs say it was the best thing that ever happened. Sometimes I have even heard people say when they have lost their husband or wife that it was the best thing that happened in their life. So, whenever you feel frightened about outcomes like losing a job or certain relationship, it is a time to go within, release the fear, and open to a deep trust that can only lead to miracles.

Living a life of devotion doesn't mean dropping responsibilities. The practice is to trust that you can be guided within your responsibilities in ways that unwind fear and control. If your beliefs are strong, they need to be seen through and handed over completely or else they will still be there percolating in the back of your consciousness, directing your thoughts and actions. And yes, devotion to God will ultimately free you completely from worldly responsibilities and concerns. You want to live your life with such devotion that you actually allow the concerns of this world to fade away. As things flow, there will be flexibility if you have trust, for example in your daily responsibilities and schedules. This is because your perception has changed, and you have opened to see things from the Holy Spirit's perspective, from deep acceptance and peace. You begin to let everything be used for this goal, for this experience of trust.

Once this link with your inner teacher is made, your way is set. You experience a clear pathway. In trust, you feel that the Holy Spirit goes before you, leading, guiding, and giving you everything to say and do, every person you are to meet, and every place you are to move. You experience your direction in life as if there is a very specific plan already available and you don't have to figure it out. You don't have to weigh the pros and cons or try to anticipate the future, and there is no need to fear it either. You move in the direction of dropping the need for personal control because you're going for an experience of letting the Holy Spirit plan and organize all things for you, relieving you from the belief that you must plan for yourself. You are relieved from this heavy burden of control, planning, and management of your life. Every second that you spend trusting will give you huge rewards: contentment and peacefulness.

Accepting everything with the Holy Spirit in your mind allows everything to be used for peace and healing. You will realize that you are not able to judge which activities and relationships are most helpful for your opening to the present. You no longer wish to play the game of pick and choose. When you trust and accept that your whole life is being given by the Holy Spirit, you enter into such receptivity and flow that you see everything as perfect support, as given just for you!

CHAPTER 8

ACCEPTANCE

When you trust with a willingness in your heart to be healed, you are open to accept anything that comes your way. But do you have to accept everything as it is in this world? After all, this world was born, quite literally, in the refusal to accept things as they are, the perfection of Heaven. There seem to be so many problems. Humanity seems to complain a lot. For example, it's very common to complain about the environment. It seems normal and reasonable to complain about loud noises, pollution, hot or cold weather, or gray skies. Because of this, it's also considered valuable and important to be an activist, to take a stand to save the environment and so forth. Apart from trying to change everything and be an activist, is the only other option to just withdraw and accept things as they are perceived, or is there a third option? Does the Holy Spirit give us another way?

The first time I was in Beijing, the person who was driving apologized for the smog and the pollution. He said, "I am so sorry that our skies are so grey," and I said, "Oh, they are beautiful. I am loving your grey skies." When people apologize for something, they wish something could be better, while I join in acceptance with what is. I joined with the grey skies. I enjoy grey skies actually, and when people ask me about pollution, I join with pollution. In my mind, I join with everything because it is all unified in my awareness. When you become all-inclusive in your wanting God or wanting peace, you have an experience that there is nothing outside, there is nothing else, and therefore, there is nothing to judge.

Pollution is entirely neutral. But when you take that concept and judge it, for example stating, "Polluted is the opposite of clean," then you project that belief, and you find evidence for your judgment. You must have judged something for any anger, irritation, and annoyance to appear. Then you see evidence of what you judged. It is simply by deciding that you do not like something that it appears on your mental screen.

If your acceptance only centers around the positives of the world, you'll be happy for a while, then the heartbreak will come in, and pain will come back. You go back and forth between heartbreak and happiness, and life is like an emotional yo-yo. But there is something inside that knows we are entitled to more than that, that we are entitled to a sense of consistency as a state of mind, peace of mind. If we live from a state of Spirit-inspired acceptance, this will unify our perception and stabilize our emotions.

Conscious acceptance therefore becomes our pathway. Conscious acceptance is a practice that leads to joy as certain as refusal to accept things as they are leads to pain and misery. In order to really understand conscious acceptance, we must understand the problem of judgment. Judgment is the birth of all perception. We have judged against God metaphysically in our belief in separation, and multiplicity and choices in form were born. That is why perception is always selective, and we seem to be able to accept what we want and reject what we do not want, usually based on the pain-and-pleasure mechanism—on subjective and personal "likes" and "dislikes." But do we really know what we want? Can we recognize that in a state of believed separation, we don't really know what we want? The foundation of our thought system is made from an original opposition against what is, and thus acceptance and awareness of That Which Is—God—has become an alien concept.

Acceptance, in the true spiritual sense, is to go within and relinquish projection and judgment by allowing external conditions to be the way they are. They are not the real problem. In this state of awareness, there is no point in complaining about pollution or bad weather. Being in this state of trust and acceptance is not a passive experience. It is very much a state of actively being present with what life presents. By living your life from a state of Spirit-inspired acceptance, you get deeper into your purpose. You realize that you will only be content with a happiness that is everlasting.

The feeling of acceptance is of a receptive mind, an open mind. It's a key characteristic for experiencing the miracle within. The miracle is basically a shift of perception from the ego's opposition to true life, to perceive everything as given for your highest good.

Merging with Everything Through Conscious Acceptance

It's wonderful when we realize that we can join in mind with anything in this universe: a sight, a sound, a memory, an object. The practice is to come back to the mind, to come to a deeper point of not knowing how or what to judge, to the place inside where we actually don't know what is good or bad. This takes you back to I-am-ness, which is prior to judgment. In that acceptance is your strength. Your invulnerability is in that being-ness, in that I-am-ness.

When we don't know the way out of our judgment, the way to our own healing is through conscious acceptance. Conscious acceptance is to step back, tune in, and let yourself be guided. Not because it is good or right, but because it is the only way that will work. You will ultimately come to a resonance with the inner guidance because that is what will set you free. It will take you back to true freedom.

It is an undeniable fact that everything works together for our good. For most of us, this is not how we experience our daily life because all ego goals—goals that are related to form, appearances, outcomes, and preferences—have nothing to do with truth or reality. We can't perceive what is in our own best interests while we go for goals and outcomes of form generated in a world of opposites and conflicts.

As mentioned in chapter 1, *A Course in Miracles* states that "in no situation that arises do you realize the outcome that would make you happy." In no situation. None! And here it is: There is never a specific outcome that would make you consistently happy—ever—because there is not one that exists. You are asked to be very sincere, to concede to this crucial realization that your general goals aren't really in your best interest. You are pursuing goals that are about survival, comfort, material gain, interpersonal love, and situations, people, places, and events to satisfy your expectations: "I will be happy when the world looks this way, when my personal life looks this way." You are simply putting your own limitations on the Divine. God is so much bigger, vaster, richer, freer, and happier than you can imagine, so wouldn't it be better to accept all that He gives, which can always only be coming from divine love?

EXERCISE: I Do Not Perceive My Own Best Interests

Take some time now to look inward, breathe, and relax, and invite the Holy Spirit to join you in preparation for your next assignment.

This exercise requires much more honesty than you may be accustomed to using. We will directly address your form- and time-based goals. They may be goals that you have given a lot of value to. Although in the light and perspective of the Spirit, they are very likely to lose a lot of their former importance. You may have noticed that you have a bunch of goals that result from ideas about how the world should work out.

Pick a couple of unresolved situations or conflicts in your life. In your journal, write down several desired outcomes that you think would help you solve those situations. The emphasis should be on uncovering the outcome that you hope for. You can, for example, use this format: "In the situation involving _____, I would like _____ and _____ to happen," and so on. You may discover that some of your desired outcomes may even conflict. The purpose of writing them down is solely to relinquish the idea that your happiness will come from your own desired outcomes. When you have searched your mind for several minutes and can't find any more desired outcomes, pause and reflect on this lesson from A Course in Miracles:

I do not perceive my own best interests.

In no situation that arises do you realize the outcome that would make you happy. Therefore, you have no guide to appropriate action, and no way of judging the result. What you do is determined by your perception of the situation, and that perception is wrong.

Now go through the following questions. Use your journal to write down your answers.

1. Did you find conflicting personal or form goals in your journal inquiry?

2. Are you able to recognize that the emphasis on outcomes is a distraction from the goal of peace of mind?

3. Are you willing to loosen from the idea that you think you know what is in your own best interest so you can learn what your best interest is?

As you explore your various goals this way, you may recognize that you are making a large number of demands of situations. You will also recognize that many of your goals are contradictory, that you have no unified outcome in mind, and that you must experience disappointment in connection with some of your goals however the situation turns out.

Now, open up to surrendering from striving to achieve these goals and satisfying your ideas about how your life should work out. The Holy Spirit is constantly inviting you to surrender this way and to accept peace of mind as your goal and sole outcome in any situation.

As a symbol of your letting go of outcomes, you could rip these pages from your journal and crumple them up. You could get a glass bowl and safely burn the pages, watching them disappear into smoke.

It takes trust to realize that you don't have to, nor can you control outcomes. Relax into the acceptance that in no situation do you know the outcome that would make you happy. Let the Holy Spirit's guidance lead you, and in acceptance, you see that you have what you always wanted—peace.

The Ease of Miraculous Flow

"What could you not accept if you but knew that everything that happens, all events, past, present, and to come, are gently planned by One Whose only purpose is your good? Perhaps you have misunderstood His plan, for He would never offer pain to you. But your defenses did not let you see His loving blessing shine in every step you ever took. While you made plans for death, He led you gently to eternal life."

We've all been through times where we cry and feel like we want to pull our hair out. But we reach a point where we can just really laugh. It just starts to get funnier and funnier. That's acceptance. That's being aligned with the Holy Spirit.

You know that you are in acceptance when you become surrendered in your life: surrendered away from opinions; surrendered away from agendas; surrendered away from trying to control the world, events, and situations. Acceptance promotes an exquisite experience of effortless flow. You can tell that you have let go of control and that you are in acceptance when you experience your life and the world with ease. If everything just seems to be in a rhythm, if everything just drops in and falls into place easily, and if you're gliding through the world, then you know that you are in acceptance.

As the trust in guidance builds, your capacity for acceptance grows, which ultimately leads to an experience that all things are equally acceptable. This state of nonjudgment means that you see and accept all things and appearances as truly helpful for your healing. This doesn't mean that you have some sort of obligation to every situation that comes your way. But your attitude becomes welcoming and open rather than suspicious to things that happen. You are developing your intuition to use discernment as you learn that everything comes your way for healing.

This state of mind leads to experiences of more and more miracles. Acceptance combined with trust is the recipe for miracles. It's inevitable that you will experience miracles once you begin to trust the flow and orchestration of all events. You have opened up to a whole different perception. You are coming to know that there is a real purpose for everything. It's like the movie *August Rush*, which is a beautiful example of how everything is orchestrated perfectly. Even when things don't look good, August stays committed to his calling and inner certainty. As for August, a genuine flow of all things becomes your natural and peaceful perception. You have met the conditions for your miracle-minded life, and love wins the day!

CHAPTER 9

PEACE OF MIND

When unconscious beliefs are not brought to the forefront of our minds to be looked at and released, the past replays itself over and over. This is no life. It is like being a robot—getting up in the morning, brushing your teeth, getting ready for work, and just going through the motions. How many of us get up in the morning, sit up in bed, and ask: "What is the nature of reality? I do not even want to brush my teeth until I get a handle on this!"

Later, you click into gear, and maybe during your lunch hour or sometime at work, you will have questions like, "What am I doing here? What is the purpose of any of this?" Often these questions get brushed aside by all the things you think you have to do, the so-called "practical things" that get in the way of investigating more deeply. But you can't get to a state of peace until you let go of the beliefs that are blocking your awareness and experience of it.

All We Need Is Willingness

We need a willingness to heal our mind. We need to be willing to see where we say no to peace. In fact, we only need willingness. We do not need intelligence, we do not need lots of money, and we do not need lots of skills and abilities—all the things that the world says are essential. In my life, I did not have a lot of money, and I did not feel like I had a lot of skills, but I know I was very, very willing to be shown, to let the doors be opened. If you come to God with willingness and sincerity, then watch out: it will knock your socks off! You will arrive at an experience of peace, freedom, and clarity that you had never imagined or ever thought was possible. You will truly know who you are.

Like I mentioned previously, the ego is bent on outcomes in form, on setting specific external goals and then striving to achieve them. In doing that, we're still not happy. Then the quest becomes, "What is next?" The game of "I will be happy when…" goes on and on. Eventually, we realize how powerful it is that peace is just a decision. Why not have peace of mind be our goal?

What We Are Really Asking For

It's not in our conscious awareness that peace is always there, rather it is buried deep within our minds, covered over by beliefs and attachments. Therefore, our way to peace must always involve the very rewarding undertaking of uncovering of beliefs.

Someone once asked me: "You say we all get what we want. I have a friend who would not agree with you. She is forty-five years old, she has always wanted a husband and a child, and she has not gotten them. She is praying, and we say to her, 'Leave it up to God,' but you say that we get things even if it's our ego that wishes it. So, what would you say to her?"

No matter what seems to be going on in specifics, on the surface, or in our hearts, we never really ask for "things." What we are really always asking for is an experience or a state of mind. You could ask your friend questions like, "What is your experience?" and if she said, "Well, I'm lonely. I want a husband and a child because I want something to fill my life up. I want a feeling of joining, of connection. I want to share my life with someone. I want to share the joys of being a parent." She could start to see that there is a belief of lack in her mind. It is this belief that leads to the experience of loneliness, feeling isolated, or feeling empty and unfulfilled. She may express things like, "Okay, I'm feeling empty, a bit alone, and unfulfilled." The way her life and the world look for her is a reflection of those feelings.

When we feel this emptiness, isolation, and loneliness, it is not the way it looks in the world that is causing us to feel this way. It is not our circumstances of being single or married, for example. We are feeling it because that is our state of consciousness. We are feeling that way because of our desire to follow ego beliefs that tell us we are capable of feeling lonely, empty, or isolated. We always get what we ask or pray for. That means we are always getting exactly what we are aligning our mind with. The form of our life is simply an out-picturing of our inner beliefs and desires, bringing witness to an inner state of mind, without exception.

So, this woman who does not want to feel lonely could start working more inwardly to cultivate the experience of a relationship with the Holy Spirit within: releasing the feelings, looking at the beliefs, looking at the thoughts that are running through her mind on a daily basis. And she eventually would say, "The good news is that I'm not a victim. I'm not powerless based on those thoughts." In fact, we are never powerless in the face of our beliefs because we can change them. We can change our minds in an instant.

She could look at how this is demonstrated in others. All of us have known or met people who are very, very happy and joyful. Some of them are what we would call single, and some of them are what we would call married. Some of them have children; some of them don't. This shows us that happiness, joy, and love are not circumstance dependent. Nothing is really dependent on the circumstances. Sometimes people can feel very lonely in a crowd, but when they are on a walk in the forest all by themselves, they feel joy and a connection to the whole universe and everyone in it.

Sometimes people say to me, "Yes, David, we see that you are very happy, but that's just because of your circumstances. If you were married, if you had children, if you had a mortgage, and if you had a boss, let's see how happy you would be then." Well, it would be really strange if God would set up a world where some people could have fortunate circumstances and other people could have unfortunate circumstances. Wouldn't it be much more reasonable to think that whatever world we are perceiving is there by our own choice? We have chosen our life the way we know it. We built it. It is like the little child with the building blocks, making a castle, making a little fort or something, building, and then looking at what has been built. There is really no point in lamenting circumstances. They are there by decision. On an unconscious level, they have been chosen. We chose everything in our movie the way we preferred it. Even if it seems undesirable to us, on some level, our ego-self wanted it that way. And, of course, this is why you can learn to choose again. You are not locked into circumstances, but by choosing peace more and more consistently, you get a whole new experience of all circumstances and situations. When the woman who feels lonely focuses on getting in touch with her core desire, the experience she wants, rather than on the external circumstances, she will find present connection and fulfillment and therefore cultivate a consistent and stable experience of peace of mind that is not dependent on outer circumstances.

The Power of Wanting

If everything that we experience is there because on some level we want it, it follows that nothing that we experience is apart from our wanting it that particular way. Thus, instead of dwelling on weakness, it is important to see how powerful our mind is. Even what we call chitter-chatter, the crazy static in the mind that you've been telling to just go away, has its powerful effects on the way we perceive the world around us.

Once we start to acknowledge the power of our wanting and the power of our prayer, then we can start to go deeper inward, asking, "Hmmm… What is it really that I want? What is my priority?" As we go deeper inward with that, we start to realize that we really want to use the power of our wanting and direct it toward peace of mind. What trinkets of the world could you possibly want if you had the option of choosing peace of mind? Everlasting peace! I had a friend who once asked me, "If I open my mind to God, can I still have my Maserati?" I said "Well, you just have to get really clear about what matters most to you. What do you really, really want?" Once you get into the power of your wanting, you start to use discrimination. And that is where we're going, to that zone of discernment, funneling more and more to a place of realizing, "Oh, I want a state of mind. What I really want is the peace of God."

To say the words, "I want peace," actually means nothing. But to mean them is everything. We need to be in touch with what we want because there are no spiritual clichés or phrases that can magically bring us real peace. Like Dorothy in *The Wizard of Oz*, all that she had to do was click her heels together, the little ruby red slippers, three times, and say the words, "There's no place like home," to go home! In one sense, Glinda the Good Witch is the Holy Spirit speaking, "You always had the power to go Home," and that is true. But "wanting peace" is really beyond a catchphrase, knowing the right mantra, or saying the right words in just the right way. The experience of peace is not found in some "abracadabra" where we've got to say just the right words to unlock the spell. Instead, we have to cultivate the good habit of turning to our heart within and really being sincere about this wanting. Ask your heart, "What is it that I really, really want?" We don't get to Heaven when we die, because Heaven is a state of mind, a state of peace that is available in the present.

A Present Peace

Once we do our inner inquiry, we can open up to the choice for real peace. This is a perspective that veers away from modern forms of spirituality that often focus on "creating your own reality or manifesting!" It differs from many of the psychotherapies and counseling practices that guide you into your past to get in touch with unconscious memories and events that are believed to be the cause of your problems. The truth is, nothing in your past or your future is causing any problem. This may seem radical to you, especially if you have focused on, and even gotten in touch with, painful memories or trauma. Unveiling repressed memories can be a very important stepping-stone in your healing and is not to be disregarded. These memories can be essential inroads to the deeper healing of your mind and opening in awareness. But remember: your egoic mind wanted every experience it ever had, and now the best you can do is to let those experiences be your inroads to the fundamental problem of separation, to heal your way back to who you really are.

The discovery of the power of our mind is essential in learning to see that our thoughts always give us an experience of either peace or turmoil. Peace of mind—as well as guilt, fear, and anger—is based on a present decision, a decision you are making this very instant. Instead of going on a witch-hunt into your past, or trying to affirm a better future, the focus is on a present decision for peace.

In A Course in Miracles, Jesus says: "One thing you must learn about the goals the ego has given you, is that when you have achieved them they have not satisfied you." Think of all the goals we set. We are told that goal setting is good, right? So, what are you if you don't have any goals? A lazy, no-good, rotten bum! Now, you are working with the Course, and what is it asking you to do? Give up all of the goals! Living as if you are giving up all of your goals except for the one single goal of present peace can take a while. We associate goals with the future, so present peace feels like a very different kind of goal. That's why it can be a bit difficult in the beginning. Also, you can bank on hearing the ego say, "Oh, come on, what a waste! You could be doing something really productive. Present peace?" That's what you will have to face. And, as long as you entertain that doubt thought, guess what? The world is going to act it out for you. It might be from your parents, your neighbors, or your spouse, "What? What's your goal? Your goal is present peace?" Anyone can act it out for you because the world you perceive is a reflection of your beliefs. So, if you have doubt thoughts about present peace, guess where they're going to show up: everywhere!

When we accept that it is our divine birthright to be in a consistent state of peace, we are taken in a whole new direction. We start to acknowledge our true strength, and that strength is freedom. The thoughts of the ego, the thoughts of temptation, can't ever enter our pristine, holy mind here. The light becomes so strong and so bright that the thoughts of the ego can't even enter!

Being Vigilant for Peace

Along the way, there are many instances where we can watch how part of our mind wants to stray away from the peace we are beginning to get in touch with. These moments of the journey are important as they are opportunities to allow the fear to come up while still being able to follow what our hearts are really telling us to do. As we trust the voice inside, or the feeling inside our heart, we strengthen our trust in our direction toward peace.

This world is made up of countless distractions and temporary pleasures to feel good for a short period of time. When we realize that indulging in temporary pleasure is an obstacle to a state of consistent peace, we recognize that we need to take a deep look at what we choose on a day-to-day, moment-to-moment basis. Our true purpose is to be happy, not to achieve things or accumulate possessions. Understanding that leads to peace of mind. The experience of freedom is of the mind and not circumstance dependent in any way.

We can get clear on what the ego is and then pull our mind back from it, reclaiming the peace in the present moment. In other words, take the juice away from the ego and reclaim the power of the mind by consistently choosing peace. For as long as we think the ego has something of value to offer us, our minds will be deprived of peace. We need to be very vigilant not to make any exceptions. Nor should we accept that there is any order of difficulty in any problem that we encounter: an illusion is an illusion regardless of its seeming magnitude. When we go deeper, we realize that we can only give up what was never real anyway. We come to see the false as false and illusion as illusion. When the resistance to peace has been removed, the light of Spirit shines unobstructed in awareness.

What makes peace of mind possible is trust in the Holy Spirit. Trusting in past learning and constructs of linear time means that there is a fear of Spirit, a fear of the higher realms, a fear of love. So, to the extent that you want to hold on to past learning, you will not be able to rest in present peace. These are the phases most of us go through before arriving back at peace:

1. First come your likes and your dislikes. You start to become aware of them and see how you would like more of your likes and less of your dislikes.

2. Then you go a little further and start to feel that your mind is powerful and that you can draw forth more of what you like and less of what you do not like (manifesting).

3. Then you go even a little higher, and you start to realize that your mind is very powerful; it is the maker of this dream.

4. When you start to realize you thought you liked this and you did not like that, but you really do not know what you want, it gets humbling. Now you are open to peace of mind and to being given an experience that is from far beyond your past learning. You start to use your powerful mind to experience only what you truly want: peace of mind.

The Only Answer Is Peace

The only way to experience this world accurately and peacefully is as a unified whole. But this is generally not our experience when we deal with everyday problems and situations. Think of the 1,001 experiences you've had recently. If you split one of these experiences off and think that there's something wrong with it or that something could have been better or different, then you're seeing with the ego, which always tries to solve situations through splitting off. I call this *fragmentation*.

If a money pit of a house had 142 problems and every one of those problems were solved, as long as you hold on to a perspective of fragmentation, there are going to be more problems. But when the purpose is changed to peace and to truth, the entire perspective of the universe is transformed. Even if the problems seem to continue, we will not experience them from a perspective of fragmentation, and we will not see them as fragmented issues in and of themselves. If we are focused only on the release of the blocks to peace of mind, we will experience a flow of guidance as to how to deal with each and every problem that appears. We will see problems as just a movie script playing out on a screen, bringing us back to peace. We will no longer want to give our power away to anything that takes away our peace. Thus, we have completely changed our perspective.

Since the problem is in the mind, it can only be resolved in the mind. The ego made the world to generate specific problems that have no answers. It generates impossible problems with no true solutions.

If we give our mind over to the Holy Spirit and inquire about a whole new way of seeing—a new vision—then we're really going inward toward the real solution. We are here to come back to a peaceful foundation and experience. It is very practical. We just need to trust and be willing to unlearn things and ideas that we thought were solid facts about ourselves and the world. The outcome is a tranquil mind. Peace of mind is not a small gift to yourself—it's everything. Can you imagine what it would be like to be perfectly peaceful, calm, and tranquil always? That is what time is for—to learn just that and nothing more. You can allow yourself to be open-minded and flexible about things as you get deeper and deeper into your practice. You can be very allowing and very peaceful.

Setting the Goal to Achieve Peace

There is a section in A *Course in Miracles* called "Setting the Goal" that explains that if you put the goal of peace out in front in each situation, you will perceive everything and everyone as supporting this goal. Setting the goal of peace is something that we can do at the very beginning of any activity. The value of deciding for peace in advance is simply that you will perceive the situation as a means to make it (peace of mind) happen. This means that perception no longer needs to be the determiner of our state of mind.

When you set your mind in advance, you focus your mind on what you want. This is the way to use time for healing purposes. The separated mind believes in the past, the present, and the future even though the eternal now is really all there is. Believing that problems are caused by past events panders to the ego's idea of separation and distracts the mind from being present in the moment. Peace is really a present choice, and believing that past events can affect or prevent you from experiencing peace right now is but a defense against the present moment. When your mind is aligned with peace as your one goal, you cannot help but see the cosmos as unified and therefore peaceful. This shows how powerful your mind really is! It shows how important it is to focus on what you truly want, on that which is truly helpful to you.

EXERCISE: Choosing Peace of Mind

To listen to a recorded version of this exercise, go to http://www .newharbinger.com/41870.

Make sure you have some time to yourself as this exercise requires deep inquiry. You may have come to a beautiful place in your journey with this book, or the journey may have started to bring up deep beliefs and even discomfort. This is okay and part of the journey. Sit comfortably now. Take a deep breath. Reflect for a moment on what you have learned from the previous chapters—guidance, trust, and acceptance—before going into the following exercise. Use your journal for free association.

1. Recall a recent situation when you felt stressed, for example when you were stuck in traffic, at work, or at home with your family. Now take some time to reflect and ask yourself these questions: What perspective did I choose in that situation? Was I choosing pain and conflict, or was I choosing peace and joy? Recall your thoughts and feelings.

   Begin to consider that you have options and that you can always choose again. In order to undo the tendency to jump into past thinking in stressful situations, this practice of considering your options rather than being reactive invites you to be vigilant with your thoughts, which is imperative when you want to achieve a state of peace.

2. What in your mind or life right now is causing you anxiety or stress? Write down at least three or four situations that are causing you concern, worry, or stress.

   These situations don't have the power to cause you to feel the way that you feel. All power lies in your own thinking. Therefore, examine any thoughts associated with the situations.

Are you blaming external circumstances for your stress? Are you willing to take responsibility for your state of mind?

Your answers to these questions will determine how quickly you will experience peace of mind.

I encourage you to make a firm commitment to the practice of going within to release the feelings and emotions that arise in stressful situations. For example, when you notice some worry, immediately pause and allow the feeling to be fully released. Remind yourself that your healing is inevitable and that peace of mind is available right now. Realize that it's all for your healing, rather than something that is happening *to* you.

In an unexpected situation, you may catch yourself feeling irritated by outside surroundings, or you may feel annoyance or impatience. This is your opportunity to step back and pray for a miracle. Ask yourself: "Do I believe this annoyance has external causes? Or am I now beginning to recognize my own reactions and interpretations?" Remind yourself that it is with acceptance, regardless of how difficult the situation seems to be, that you can peacefully go through it. Join with the true prayer of your heart and ask for help from your inner guide, the Holy Spirit.

This practice requires willingness and vigilance, and your peace of mind is more than worth it. Start now. Know that true peace of mind is the only experience that is real and ultimately inevitable.

Prayer: Only Peace Remains

Take some time now to relax and just be, in this moment, sincerely, with the Holy Spirit as a loving presence to comfort and guide you. Allow yourself to rest deep within the core of your being while you read the following prayer:

As I sink inward,
I begin to see the nature of the mind,
and the powerful nature of thought.

When I accept God's freedom for myself,
I accept God's freedom for everyone and everything,
because there is nothing outside of mind.

As I change my mind, the entire world looks different,
as I accept the Spirit's vision I can see.

No longer will I confuse pain and joy.
Pain is the outcome of the ego; joy is the inspiration of Spirit.

The confusion between pain and joy is the cause of any suffering
and if I follow the Holy Spirit, the ego will be given up,
and I will suffer nothing.

I will, instead, be gaining everything: joy, true freedom, and
inner peace.
This is my choice.

Now I accept the will of God,
and I accept that God's will is my will.

There is nothing else.

This is peace.

Amen.

The Observing Mind

Raising unconscious beliefs to awareness is deep, inner work. It takes a lot of willingness and humbleness. This is why affirmations don't really work. For example, affirming that you are loved, loving, and happy without taking a deep look at the darkness and self-hatred is nothing more than a temporary fix that, at best, can spur your inspiration to take it a bit deeper.

In my own life, the parable of David, going within and facing the emotions whenever I felt uncomfortable that I wasn't with somebody and feeling the discomfort of aloneness was a very important part of emptying my mind of all concepts and coming to inner peace. You may have had the experience of feeling lonely in a crowd or the feeling of connectedness when you're walking alone along the beach, for example. Such experiences give a hint that everything is really about your psychological state of mind. So, it comes down to a lot of practice, emptying, and clearing to get down to what's under the little nudges that you feel. There's a root that runs much deeper, the root that takes you down into the guilt experience. Whenever I've looked for completion in partnership, in work, in family relationships, in environmental situations, and in different locations and countries, I discovered that it didn't work. Those things weren't lasting, and they didn't offer a sense of completion and peace of mind. Instead, I have come to a clear awareness that there is a purpose, a calling that's in me, that is identical to this ever-present moment. The spiritual journey is really about finding your inner calling and then following it. Because when you do that, it takes you into an extraordinary state of mind that is actually very natural, for its very nature is peace.

You may start to see that the way to experience peace is through just observing the world. Sinking back into the soft and gentle presence of the observer is the whole purpose of the spiritual journey. Being the observer and being able to watch it all, to not get caught in the mortal fuss, and to not even have an opinion about it or to feel that you have to participate in it is your goal. When you are in Spirit, you are really beyond the touch of time. Time goes by without its touch upon you. You aren't really a traveler through time and space, but you travel through ideas, concepts, and beliefs until you reach the shore of tranquility, of deep peace.

PART III

MIRACLES IN

RELATIONSHIPS

CHAPTER 10

TRANSFORMING SPECIAL RELATIONSHIPS

As you get closer to your true desire for peace, you will find it important to look at your relationships. Your relationships are mirrors to your mind, to what you believe. The greatest barometer for your state of mind is found in the way you feel in all of your relationships, be they close intimate ones, family, friends, colleagues and business associates, or casual encounters. The closer the relationship, the deeper the healing potential, so in this chapter, I'll talk about "special" relationships. Whenever we think of ourselves as special, the ego has us look for what is different or lacking in others. The ego then compares, making us better, or more special, than the "other." This judging is what the ego considers its job. At the most basic level, specialness is a belief in differences. This belief will always be the cause of distress and conflict in relationships because it is based on separation. This chapter will unveil the dynamics of specialness and how the ego uses it in relationships.

Most people think of an interpersonal relationship as some kind of fulfillment because they feel that there is something empty, like a hole inside. It's common to think that a relationship will answer the call for intimacy, connection, and love. When there is this sense of need or lack in the mind, it turns into an often-unconscious desire: "I need to get something from you." This sets up a big expectation. Disillusionment is an inevitable result of the pattern of using relationships to solve a perceived inner lack or emptiness.

Maybe the most common unquestioned expectation, one that is lifted up in society, is the marriage vow. There is an expectation of longevity, where silver, gold, and diamond anniversaries are regarded as respected accomplishments. When we look outside for a partner to meet our needs and they fail to live up to the role the ego assigned to them, then it is curtains down. It is either "I've had enough of this," or we begin an ego bargaining, such as people pleasing, which just muddies the water even more, and it is not experienced as a good situation. Relationships can also be misused by the ego for projecting our emotions onto the other and blaming. "I would be happy except that you do this and this and this." Projections come flooding out. Anger and guilt need a target because it feels intolerable to own them. But we do not realize that projecting onto and blaming our partner actually keep these negative emotions alive.

Sometimes loneliness and abandonment issues are reasons why people either enter into or avoid relationships. Everyone wants intimacy, but everyone also wants freedom. We usually seek intimacy in a relationship, but when we believe this means we will lose some kind of freedom, we may end the relationship.

A relationship can be a tremendous mechanism for healing if we are willing to use it that way. A relationship offers countless opportunities to take projection back when we feel irritated, or annoyed, or even irked at mannerisms or the tiniest things.

From Specialness to Love's True Nature

When we want something from another, it is impossible to allow them to be who they really are. But this is the human condition: a state of desire or attachment to a certain idealized form. When the mind is asleep, it is desperate for innocence and love since it thinks it has lost it. As long as the ego is guiding us in our relationships, we are trying to find fulfillment and satisfaction in a form, in a body. It is as if you took a photograph and said to God, "I want one of these. I will be happy when my life looks like this." But these forms are idols, and we will never be completely fulfilled by them. You could say that Heaven's oneness, or the present moment, is a perfect state of desireless contentment. It is not wanting or needing anything, not hoping something would be different or better. It's not looking for answers. It's a state that simply is. Metaphysically, it is actually impossible to find love interpersonally or with anything "external." The only true love is the love of Spirit within.

As long as we are afraid, believing we are a separate identity, we will keep attempting to find this love outside. A common question is whether it's the ego that's behind our attraction to another person. Indeed, the ego does speak first—and loudest! The ego is impetuous and impulsive; it wants immediate gratification on its own terms. But the Spirit can use the attraction beautifully when you allow yourself to go toward a relationship and use it for healing the mind. Hanging in there in a committed relationship and facing the shadows when they come up will offer you a far deeper opportunity for the healing of your mind. Heart openings and experiences of falling in love are always helpful and will ultimately lead to an awareness of true love.

Since true love and intimacy can only be found within, you may wonder what it is that the mind is actually looking for and what a special relationship actually is. When you enter into a special relationship, you likely bring all of your old thoughts and associations with you. When you interact with a person, you're interacting with a bit of your own past. The body that you think you are and the body that you're in a relationship with are like holographs acting out of your unresolved issues.

Relationships offer a mirroring that helps you get in touch with what's going on in your consciousness, which is why they can be so intense. All personal relationships have the potential to trigger different forms of grievances like, "You said you would do this, and you didn't; you aren't the same as when I married you." Money issues, sex, jealousies, envy, and all the so-called problems within relationships, no matter how you define the situation, are based on past conditioning. The past is over, and so are the issues, but to the extent that you still believe in them, this partner is going to do you a favor and act them out in front of you. One day, you wake and say to your partner, "You believe what?" Or there could be 348 consecutive days of bliss, but then there is a trigger, and BOOM! A button-pusher. Why? Because you believe something from the past is still current. What is the other person really acting out? They're acting out the judgments and the preferences in your unconscious. This is why you're drawn more to some bodies than to other bodies, and from the Spirit's perspective, the purpose is to heal those issues.

Relationships and Purpose

What you are aiming to heal together are the unhelpful dependencies and desperations rooted in a deep belief in lack. The ego always has an outcome for relationships, like staying together at any cost or making it look good on the surface, while the Spirit offers guidance for how relationships can be used from moment to moment for healing and the undoing of things such as unhealthy dependency, control, and fear of loss. The truth is that you never really need anybody in the present moment. But when you feel very drawn to someone, you can practice simultaneously tuning in to Spirit. He will use the symbol of relationship for your awakening. Falling in love with someone can be used in the truest sense to go deep within, beyond the form to the essence, to a communion experience, to a sense of total communion, synergy, and telepathy, way beyond the form.

Everyone wants a love that doesn't come to an end. Love song lyrics usually speak of "forever" and "everlasting," and the ideal of an enduring, everlasting, harmonious, continuous relationship certainly sounds good. Yet, those terms don't typically describe interpersonal relationships in this world. For even in the "best relationships," when they seem to be sustained, it is still perceived that death of the body, or splitting up and moving on, cuts the relationship short of the ideal. From that perspective, there seems to be an ending. When there is a breakup, there can seem to be a lack of love, a heartache. However, if a relationship seems to come to an end and you're no longer together, but the thought of that person comes into your mind all the time, then you're actually still in that relationship. Your healing and learning continue even when the bodies are no longer together. People are thoughts in your mind, and therefore, you are never left without an opportunity to heal. It takes a while before you will become good at being aware of your thoughts. I call that practice mind watching. The temptation is to only watch your mind at certain times and then slip back into mindlessness. Yet, this mind watching, especially within your relationships, is one of the major functions in returning again and again to the present moment.

Love is, in truth, always beyond form. While special love in relationships is defined by the purpose and form it takes, divine love has no limits. It is pure spirit. Freedom and intimacy can only be found by going inward, no matter if you are single or in a relationship. You'll experience this truth only when you are free of attachment to outcomes and as you allow the Holy Spirit to remove the limits that you place on the sharing and extending of your love.

Moving Toward Holy Relationship

It is a blessing that we can use all of our relationships to see where we need healing of our minds and where we still have grievances. Even in a special relationship, Spirit, when invited in, can help us see and guide us in what must be released in our mind through watching what our partner is mirroring back to us.

One time when I was in Argentina, some friends took me to watch professional tango. The dancers were slicing through the air, enacting all the drama of relationships. They slice so fast because there're all kinds of relationship-related passion and emotions in the dance. There's even a history of murder associated with the tango. So, under that slicing, there's a little bit of "I could kill you." Their faces are very expressive and very dramatic. There's a lot of the drama and the trauma of special relationships under those whisking bodies cutting through the air. Everybody on Earth can relate to the intense emotions in relationships. The ego gets flushed out of its unconscious hiding place. It comes up to the surface, and it is vicious. What was passion, romance, and attraction seem to easily turn into hatred.

A Course in Miracles has nine chapters dedicated to special relationships! In special relationships in this world, it slips back and forth between, "I love you, I love you, I love you; and I could kill you!" The rage and the passion are a razor blade's width apart. So close. If that's the case, how can a special relationship become the means to enlightenment, to spiritual awakening? It is through forgiveness in day-to-day living. We can be grateful to all the people in our life because they reveal our grievances to us.

As you take steps toward accepting the true purpose of all of your relationships, you need to not only put your mind into it; you need to live it. Imagine being a mathematician who never wanted to practice with equations or an auto mechanic who didn't get under the hoods of cars. Imagine a bricklayer who couldn't stand mortar and bricks; you would laugh! In the same way, as humans, we need to awaken by relating to and looking at our relationships with people.

"Have no expectations" is the way of allowing things to be exactly as they are. It takes a lot of clearing the filter of consciousness to come to that state of mind. I performed a wedding where the couple's vow was "I love you now," which I thought was a wonderful vow. They were very mindful of the trap of future expectations. They wanted to allow the relationship to be used by the Holy Spirit for holiness, to clear the mind of any subtle expectations.

For me, the most helpful answer from A Course in Miracles came when I was guided to leave a relationship. I had a tremendous amount of hurt and pain around the idea of leaving. I was facing fear of abandonment. I had the Course in my hand, and I prayed to the Holy Spirit, "Please, you must answer me before I can do this." I then opened the book to the section on relationships in the Manual for Teachers. My eyes went straight to a sentence that said, "Each teaching-learning situation is maximal in the sense that each person involved will learn the most that he can from the other person at that time." Suddenly, my heart lifted. I felt that the Holy Spirit was saying, "It's okay; you and your partner learned as much as you could learn in that relationship." He was saying, "Job well done. You did a very good job, and I will be with you in your next relationship." This gave me the permission to go on and take the next step.

As you move toward holy relationships, the ego will come at you pretty strongly to try to break your turn toward healing. It will try to sabotage and abort the mission of healing by intensifying the mirroring.

But that's where I encourage you to just hang in there and ask for Spirit's help. The breakthrough will be in overcoming the ego's attempt and the longing to objectify and localize love and its attempt to shrink it from the vastness that it is. Overcoming this obstacle is the undoing of the special love relationship and the transition into holy relationship.

Giving your relationships a holy purpose is the means to reaching the transcendent perspective that looks upon bodies much like dancing leaves in the wind on a fall day. With a little wind blowing the leaves around, you notice with detachment all the colors. You're not saying, "Red, orange, brown, green." You're watching the swirl from a place of complete nonjudgment. And that's what holy relationship is. As you go about your daily relationships, be alert to temptations to:

- desire perfection in another's behavior

- blame and emphasize flaws and inconsistencies, either aloud or silently

- make comparisons

- want to be right at the expense of your brother or sister's innocence.

When you join with another in the purpose of healing the mind, you find love. Practice turning your attention to:

- examining ego thoughts and patterns within your own mind, so that they can be seen and healed

- allowing your relationships to show you what needs to be healed within your own mind

- looking beyond form and behaviors in your relationships

- releasing judgments and comparisons

- practicing defenselessness in your communications

- having peace as your goal in your joining with others and the world

- seeing the gift in practicing the above!

EXERCISE: Undoing Specialness

The following exercise aims at helping you become more aware of your part in building obstacles and issues in a relationship. It will help you see that you can change your experience with a relationship solely by looking at your own mind, and not hiding and protecting, but lifting reactions, judgments, and hidden opinions to the Holy Spirit.

Part 1: Observe Your Patterns in Relationship

You are now going to identify what obstacles are in the way of your experience of holy relationship. Let the following questions draw out some of your past and present relationship experiences. Let a relationship come to mind in which you are seeking something from another. Go inward and journal what comes to mind as you answer each question.

1. What specifically are you seeking?

2. Can you see whether this pursuit is based upon a belief in lack of some kind?

3. Looking back over your life, do you notice any patterns, repeating circumstances, or persistent feelings, such as being responsible; feeling needy, dependent, rejected, or letdown; or taking control or being controlled?

4. What beliefs do you feel might be underneath these patterns? For example, if you've felt either dependent or controlling in your relationships, is there a belief that you are helpless?

5. Can you begin to see how you are projecting your beliefs onto the other (for example "You aren't good enough") when, really, it is a belief you hold about yourself ("I'm not good enough")?

6. What do you believe you could gain or lose through the relationship? Observe your thoughts and beliefs.

7. How would you feel and what do you think your life would be like without those thoughts and beliefs?

Take a breath and for the next few minutes, in prayer, direct your mind toward dropping these thoughts and beliefs. Having seen the thoughts and beliefs that led you to feel a sense of separation, offer them to the Holy Spirit. Now, ask for help to see your friend differently. Each of these thoughts stems from the belief that you and they are different, and that what you see and do not like about them is what you do not like about yourself. They save you from the disturbance you feel in your heart, the disturbance that was a result of withholding your love from them. Your grievance against them is now replaced with awareness and freedom. Rest within the spaciousness this release brings. Feel free to write or share about your experience to strengthen it in awareness.

When egoic patterns are seen and recognized, you can easily spot them as they recur, and you can choose again. It's the first step toward knowing an intimacy that is not of personhood but of the Spirit within.

"The Holy Spirit's temple is not a body, but a relationship."

The Blessings of Relationship

As you pivot toward healing through your relationships, you will feel grateful for the gifts they are offering. It's when you get to the point where you feel that you're not attacking or blaming another anymore that you know you have matured spiritually. It means your consciousness has expanded toward understanding that all that seems to be happening outside you actually stems from your own mind. Even in your difficult relationships, you see there are valuable lessons to learn. So, you can start to honestly ask what each relationship is showing you about your mind. And once you can see the patterns and beliefs a relationship is mirroring, then you will see the blessing and its healing potential.

We are never meant to be dependent on a relationship, but rather we are meant to find the Holy Spirit in it because, really, we all share the same purpose: to wake up. Little by little, we feel more fulfilled from this practice, fulfilled from within, and our motive for relationships turns around from trying to get things from another to seeing an opportunity to give and collaborate whereby everyone benefits!

When you are ready for this renewed purpose, you will start to move from the familiar and special relationships of the world to healed and holy relationships. The ego will still seem to come at you, but that's when Spirit is always available to help and says, "You've come this far; stay with your faith. I am with you." Your prayer to the Holy Spirit becomes, "I let Your vision take the place of my perception, which is just a presentation of the past, appearing once again as if it's still occurring."

This makes way for a new vision of love that will allow you to meet with someone anew, as if for the very first time without your beliefs from the past being projected onto them.

The miracle of relationship is a journey from specialness to holiness; from exclusivity to experiences of inclusion; and from separation, fear, and loneliness to true joining, love, and joy. It is an awakening, a shift in perception from separate interests of "me," "mine," and "what's in it for me," to a shared interest, purpose, and goal. This is how you are blessed; the more love that you let pour through you, the more aware you will be of how powerful that love is, and your relationships will flourish and expand.

It's therefore beneficial to stay open and honor the relationships that come your way however they might look initially. And, as you learn to use them in truly helpful ways, they will allow you to heal, let go of specialness, and lead you back to God.

CHAPTER 11

FROM PEOPLE PLEASING TO TRUE EMPATHY

Special relationships always entail compromise and sacrifice. The compromise comes in because of the fear of "rocking the boat." There is belief in consequences, so people pleasing becomes the general mode of operation. But denial and repression build when you do not speak what is in your heart for fear of other people's reactions. If you only live to get other people to agree with you or approve of you, you are denying what you truly feel in any given situation.

Just like the desire for specialness, people pleasing is something we do when we are feeling small and limited. The word "sorry" comes up a lot. Someone touches an elbow in a crowd by mistake, and they say, "Sorry." Someone stares at you, you glance over, and they say, "Oh, sorry, sorry." And the thought arises, *I looked at you for 7.2 seconds. Sorry, that was over the limit; it was very rude of me to stare at you.* It's like there is a giant apology going on everywhere. This is made-up social conditioning. It's an example of trying to adhere to bodies and their perceived differences. Some would say it's an example of being overly sensitive and of not wanting to be in anyone's space or doing anything that could be judged as disturbing by another. It reflects a belief that we have to limit ourselves and compromise as an attempt to fit in.

In the deceived, separate state, the mind is highly uncertain. Because we are identified as a distinct and separate person, our true strength is obscured and is something that the mind is out of touch with. Therefore, the attempt to look to people for approval or behaving in certain ways to make it smooth for others becomes a way to feel accepted, liked, and approved of. We feel okay only if we are okay to others. People pleasing is a bargain with reality. It is ego looking for love, recognition, and respect from others to consolidate the belief in a small self. It can take many forms. It can be looking up to other people or covering things over. It is a way of trying to minimize fear but without actually letting it go. While you are busy focusing on external situations, it will be difficult to find stability and peace of mind. If egocentric pride and preoccupation with self is on one end of a pendulum, then people pleasing and preoccupation with others is on the other. When we people please, we make other people so important that we lose all sense of integrity.

People pleasing is a powerful defense mechanism: It keeps true joining and authentic relationships at bay. It keeps the separation in place. It's usually heavily reinforced as being something wonderful. It is encouraged. We are raised to be people pleasers—to please our parents, our relatives, our employers, our spouses, our children.

The Fear of Rising and Speaking Up

How would our life be if we would start to speak up about what is going on in our awareness and no longer dance around our issues, if we would say what we need to say? The Bible said, "Let your yea be yea and your nay be nay." When you are very layered with people pleasing—courteous, acting nice, mild-mannered, and all that—it's hard to let your yeses be yes and your noes be no. You may say yes to many requests and invitations, and then at some point think, *What have I just agreed to? I've just planned my whole week, but I just want to rest!* We have to learn how to discern and let our yeses and noes come from a place of integrity inside where we join with the Holy Spirit and follow His guidance. This is how to be truly comfortable and free of fear of consequences!

With people pleasing, the layers come on really thick, to the point that you just freeze up. Your unconscious thoughts and beliefs don't get unlocked. No matter how hard you work at your ability to please, that "disapproving look" always comes at some point. You get that stab in the heart when you think you have disappointed someone or that you have done something terribly wrong. The guilt! "Did I let you down?" And the disapproving voice comes back with, "Yes, you did. I am disappointed with you. I thought better of you. I thought I could trust you," the words that just twist a dagger in your heart. It always comes back to get you. You walk on eggshells for years, taking great care not to upset people. You tiptoe along over all those eggshells, and then suddenly you hear one crack. Yikes! All of your efforts to please were about avoiding disapproval and disappointment. You constricted and contorted yourself into a little pretzel in order to please. But it did not work. You may continue pleasing for twenty, thirty, or fifty years without coming to a vibrant experience of what true integrity and joining really is.

In my family, we never talked about feelings—never. You might have heard the joke, "Grab it—there's a feeling loose in the living room!" Talking about feelings was just off-limits. You could talk about the weather, the sports scores, who broke up with whom, who's dating whom, and everything in between, but don't talk about the feelings! Mom and Dad never talk about their feelings. Mom and Dad don't even express affection. And you internalize that. It's just reinforced that this is the way relationships are and that you don't talk about anything that seems uncomfortable.

Why would we people please unless we were afraid of losing our relationships, our parents or children, or our jobs? Why would we people please at all? Without fear, we would just tell it like it is; we would speak from our heart. This is the starting point for freeing our minds and moving toward a state of consistent peace.

It is important to acknowledge your perceptions and your feelings because they are inroads into what's underneath. But if you're burying your authentic feelings, how are you going to get in touch with and acknowledge the thoughts and beliefs that are underneath them? (See the levels of mind discussion in chapter 2.)

People pleasing is the substitute "love" that the ego has in place of true love. It is all to do with trying to stay in your comfort zone and resisting deeper change. It is thus an insidious defense against our true Self. It comes from a desire to be liked. It often includes giving in to peer pressure. Codependency is common. People pleasing comes from a false contract in the mind, made to keep your self-concept and familiar roles. It is a way of distracting yourself by seeking to find love and recognition from others instead of from within. But it is merely self-deception.

Let's look at what people pleasing covers up in the mind. It is a subtle version of the lethal poison analogy described in chapter 4, where the ego simply dilutes the guilt so we don't notice its presence. In fact, the guilt is so diluted that people pleasing actually seems to be a good thing. People work at it for lifetimes; they try to get really good at pleasing others without recognizing that it is just guilt dressed up to look good. When you live from a self-concept, you wear a mask and play roles. This is laying a limit upon your own mind.

If you solely run your life on the surface, without getting at what is underneath, then you'll never really come to true healing. The people pleaser suppresses resentment, frustration, and other emotions while doing what they believe is expected. People pleasing thus comes from a desire to perceive oneself as a victim. It is impossible to stay a victim and not have attack thoughts toward the perceived victimizer and thus oneself.

The Refreshing Courage of Honesty

We can now challenge ourselves through mind training and mind watching. We can become really, really honest with our motivations. By looking into our minds, we can see why we reason in certain ways, notice how often there is people pleasing behind it, and stop doing things out of believed expectations. We will begin to see when, and maybe even why, we think there is gain through playing out victimhood. Refuse to be a victim of anything in this world and release all those who you assign a victimizer role. This is the master switch to the light that will shine away all darkness in the mind and remind you who you truly are.

You don't have to wear and hide behind a mask, to pretend to be happy when you feel angry. Recognizing that you are not actually a victim, you can start to cultivate willingness to expose the people-pleasing role, the mask, for it covers the present moment in awareness. In that process, you need to be straightforward and honest and practice letting your words be guided when you speak to someone. This frees you up.

People pleasing runs most interactions in daily living. Because of its hold on our personality self, we get so locked into pleasing everyone that we generally need a few jolts before we realize how pervasive the problem is. An example is that you start to have experiences of being turned away or rejected when you offer your knowledge and advice. This is because you are likely doing it where it's not asked for or wanted. We can encounter reactions that feel really awkward in the sense that people won't agree to the people-pleasing games anymore. Instead, people will start to reflect our desire to heal! Or reversed, people who expect you to play the same games will react when you stop using this habitual way of interacting. These are just events to observe, but not to get hung up on. The need to be liked is of the ego. Spirit-inspired courtesy doesn't require that approval from others, rather it encourages you to follow your heart.

The ego is saying that you cannot just wake up to happiness and peace because there are other people to deal with whom you are responsible for. The fear of letting someone down is tied with believing that you are someone in the world and part of someone else's dream. The truth is that you are the dreamer of the dream in its totality.

Moving Toward True Empathy

Through conditioning, it is believed normal and even expected to empathize with someone around a perceived problem if something bad happens to them or if they are sick. When wearing the mask of a kind person, you will use phrases like, "Oh, that is terrible! You poor person! Oh, I cannot believe that happened to you! Is it not a shame? Is it not too bad?" It's commiserating with something that's just an error in perception. So, being "kind" this way is actually an attempt to make the error real, to join in error. Trying to understand and let others know how sorry you feel for them quite frankly is another way of saying, "I'm better off than you." This is not true empathy, but a false way of joining.

Problems can never really be understood. They just need to be seen as they are—an error in thinking, an error in perception, coming from false beliefs or guilt, and so forth. To have true empathy is to align with the truth in your mind and in another. It brings your perception to the Holy Spirit's interpretation. It's starting to see things from the Holy Spirit's perspective.

Practicing true empathy can be challenging because there are so many temptations. When we want to fix or change somebody or when we want a situation to be a certain way, we can be sure that we have fallen into the trap of false empathy and people pleasing. When we do that, we are actually hoping to change an outside circumstance in order to resolve an inner conflict in our own mind.

It doesn't matter if you are talking to your mother, your wife or husband, your child, your neighbor, or someone you met on the street or in a restaurant. Practice by aligning with the strength of love and truth in you and allow yourself to relate to another from that place. From this perspective, you will recognize the love and truth in the other, which is usually truly empowering for them. They will feel safe with you.

This is how we build true and deep relationships. I have heard people say that practicing true empathy helps them find real friends, ones who are willing to look at their own minds and join in a healing journey. They also share that sometimes friends who only wanted their false empathy have fallen away.

Imagine living your whole life from a very intuitive, guided place where you only want the highest good for everyone, which includes your own happiness and freedom. From this place, you don't try to smooth things over or make things work out. Sometimes issues come up, in job situations for example. Something just doesn't feel right, ethically or morally, yet because of a fear of being fired, you find yourself doing certain things against your true will. Rather than taking a deep look at your belief in an outside authority, you may do things because you think you must or should. Fear of particular future events and outcomes, paired with past conditioning, dominate your thinking. You have been trained to live for an outside world, to please, to do good, to succeed.

As you mind matures, you will find yourself starting to question this conditioning and find that you want a more inspired and loving way to live. You will no longer want to appease the external world out of fear. Learning to follow your true heart's calling will not necessarily please everyone on the planet, but that shouldn't hold you back!

Giving from Your Heart

The opposite of people pleasing is true giving. What differs is your motive. True giving is motivated by joy, an overflow of inspiration, and a desire to extend. We all know how it gets in interdependent relationships, where you are walking a fine line, trying to keep the balance of give-and-take. You need to wash away this idea of reciprocity by truly giving the love that's in your heart without expectation and without exception.

To do so, let go of the fear that you could lose something. Let go of the belief that you need special affiliations with certain people or groups. When you get in touch with your truly inspired purpose, things may fall away, but it will not matter, as you will feel that you have outgrown them. You don't have to try to stretch anything or compromise, and you don't have to play to the crowd. Follow your passion and your calling—that strong feeling of what it is that you have to give and how to extend it. This draws the mind away from past patterns and associations. It is very freeing.

The story of Jesus shows us how to do this. Jesus had an attitude of love and respect without people pleasing at all. He had only true empathy and true compassion. I cry when I read the sermons Jesus gave. I cry when I see how he was interacting with his fellow human beings, no matter who they were or what they seemed to have done. We are all touched by how he treated the Samaritan woman at the well and the prostitute that they caught and were ready to stone.

Most human beings deal with a lot of compliments and criticisms as part of daily life. Even though Jesus was living with the twelve apostles, he never said, "Hey James, I like that haircut," or "Hey Peter, that's a beautiful robe you're wearing. Hey John, where did you get those sandals? They look great!" We laugh at that because those aren't Jesus's words. Yet, we often buy into compliments and criticisms in our own life. Compliments are generally judged to be positive, and the criticisms are negative. But Jesus and the Holy Spirit draw away from both of those, from judgment into a state of perfect equality, a state of grace.

We see in the world exactly what we project from our unconscious mind. Everything we think is teaching the whole universe what we believe we are and what we believe it is. Every single thought, every single word, and every single action is teaching. It's as if you were broadcasting or live streaming to the entire cosmos all the time. Projection makes perception. The world reflects your consciousness. This is why, in order to dismantle your people-pleaser habit, you need to go through a purification of consciousness, where you begin to realize how powerful your mind is.

Jesus had gone through this purification; that's why he is an example. I see him as a representation, a demonstration of the highest that we can attain in awareness. Jesus wasn't struggling and getting into all kinds of conflicts and competitions; he didn't compare and contrast or fight against anything. He had a presence that radiated, and this is a wonderful example of our natural state of mind—of gentleness, kindness, friendliness, openness, and love, all the things we would expect from a living demonstration of Spirit. It's in the day-to-day, moment-by-moment living attitude that we can demonstrate that pure love too.

Years ago, when I started undoing people pleasing and practicing true empathy, I noticed that guidance was essential. I'd be getting into these deep mystical states while meditating, and my mother would invite me to family dinners and different things. I would usually be guided to respond with something like, "Thank you very much for thinking of me; thank you so much for inviting me." The graciousness of the Spirit was always there with a thank-you, and then, "No, I don't think I'm going to be coming." Or sometimes it would even be, "I'll just have to be in the moment. I will let you know." I was living more in the moment instead of doing a lot of planning. I was allowing myself to be spontaneous and just let the Holy Spirit guide me moment by moment. I started to more and more consistently follow what I truly felt was in my heart.

By letting go of the people-pleaser role, you step into your authenticity, your true nature. You have integrity, having gone through a process of discernment. You are going to say no at times. You need to say no to loved ones. Are you ready? Are you prepared? If you really want to move beyond the ego's defenses, beyond people pleasing, get ready to say no to loved ones—as guided. And get ready to say yes—as guided. When you say no, let the Holy Spirit say it through you. It will usually come out something like, "No, thank you," or "No, but thank you so much for asking." It is a beautiful expression of love when you can say no while feeling gratitude in your heart. You are laying aside the ego's voice that insists that no is bad and yes is good. No one comes to peace of mind by people pleasing, by saying yes to everything. Jim Carrey's character in the movie *Yes Man* had to learn this!

If you have a situation where you feel you have been compromising and you need to take action, do so when you are in a state of peace. A woman who had been compromising and "pleasing" her mother with certain behaviors for thirty years recognized this defense mechanism and had an open, direct talk with her mother. The theme of the talk was "no more." The straightforward, direct approach may seem to make waves initially, but it is an antidote to denial, repression, and resentment.

Spirit-inspired courtesy is not people pleasing. So, question your thoughts and behavior and be aware of your motive. You will know by how you feel if you are people pleasing. Guilt is always hidden in the past, and you cannot have both ego-induced politeness and freedom at the same time. The present moment is forgotten when we operate from people pleasing based on past conditioning and so is the Spirit's guidance. Do not think you can hold onto the past and expect yourself to feel infinite and free at the same time. Instead, be Spirit-inspired in terms of real kindness. From this place, you do not have a moment of doubt, and there are none of those words that are in the grey zone. The results of laying aside people pleasing are authentic relationships, real healing, and joy!

You will feel a calm assurance when you speak from your heart and say what you feel is truly most helpful. As you do, past patterns, habits, and people-pleasing thoughts of guilt will dissolve away, for they were never truly a part of the real you.

EXERCISE: Your Fear of Authenticity

Bring to mind an area in your life, a relationship, or a situation where you feel that you are wearing a mask or you are afraid to "rock the boat." Take some time with your journal to reflect upon your feelings around this situation.

1. Write down your thoughts and judgments of yourself or others. Do you have expectations of yourself or of others?

2. Look for a limiting belief about yourself. Give examples of how it is playing out in this situation.

3. Are you able to see that limiting beliefs about yourself are the cause of your people-pleasing habits?

4. Write down any ways you resist letting go of your people-pleasing habits and this limiting belief about yourself. How do you feel about letting the people-pleasing habits go? Do you want to be right about the way you perceive this situation and yourself?

5. Invite the Holy Spirit into this situation to help you release any feelings of responsibility or guilt that accompany the people pleasing and to let go of any expectations of yourself and others. If it feels effortless and natural, share with the Holy Spirit in your journal about your people-pleasing habits and your willingness to let them go and be happy.

Tips for Undoing People Pleasing

Here are some stepping-stones to help loosen your automatic people pleasing.

- When you are asked a question, instead of responding immediately, out of habit, pause. If there is a sense of pressure, defensiveness, or a lack of clarity about what you should answer, give yourself permission to say, "I don't know right now, but I will get back to you." This allows the space to really feel clear on your answer, as well as to see the ego motivation behind automatic responses. Pausing allows the space for the Spirit's guidance to be revealed.

- Be prayerful about making commitments. Giving yourself the space to feel things out and looking at your motivation before saying yes can help make the Holy Spirit's guidance more clear to you. When you have been prayerful about a decision, stick with it and follow it through.

- Speak from your heart! When you directly share your thoughts and feelings, notice any concerns about the other person's reactions. Notice and allow your fears and thoughts to arise, such as the fear of rejection, of hurting others' feelings, or of being perceived as unkind. Release these thoughts and beliefs from your mind and experience the freedom to express truthfully.

The more we work with letting go of people pleasing, we actually see that it is valuable for us to extend the truth inside of us and that really nothing's going to come down on us, the sky isn't going to cave and fall in on us. It's quite the opposite. We get a lot of opportunities on a daily basis to be vigilant around people pleasing and to allow the Holy Spirit to help us navigate our mind and the world around us. The more we communicate truly, the more we attract true communication toward us, and that is what leads us to an experience that turns fear into freedom.

The Delight of Authentic Sharing

Rather than living in fear of the possible reactions of others, we become authentic and stay in integrity with the truth. We extend the love and the happiness. We are empowered by love. From that clarity, the direction can only be integrity of mind, where everything we desire is in alignment with God, with our right-mindedness.

Living a life of no people pleasing is delightful. Doubt and worry disappear. It is peaceful; it is harmonious; it is restful. It has all the strength, the power, and the glory of the universe behind it. There is a sense of invulnerability and fearlessness. You do not hesitate. It is gentle too. It is pure light!

This is worth every bit of mind training. It is worth every bit of meditation. It is worth every bit of darkness that seems to come up in your face. It is worth it all because the reward is so great: freedom from worry. You are peaceful when you don't have a worry or a concern and the world seems to rest in peace with you. That is worth every instant of mind watching. Peace of mind is no small reward, and it is worth going for with all your heart.

CHAPTER 12

COMMUNICATION

Learning to live in the moment together with letting go of people pleasing will have a major impact on the quality of your communication with others. When your purpose is to align with Spirit, you will find that many of your experiences and activities will be reordered, renewed, and refreshed. Healing and communication are directly related, as you will discover.

When we think of communication, we usually see it as being between two people, between two bodies. One form of communication is to feel somebody's touch, hug, or caress. Another form of communication is sitting together having a cup of tea or coffee and a very intimate talk about your deepest thoughts and feelings. But even when the other person is not with you, you can communicate. Your thoughts are powerful, and anytime you think of another person, you communicate. It's like prayer. I sometimes tell people who have someone who's not around anymore, "Well, you might as well keep talking to them because they are still there. You just can't see them, but they are still there." And if you have attack thoughts toward somebody, you will see that person as the thoughts you have about them. It may feel like a very foreign idea, but it is within your own thinking that you have all of your relationships and your communications. This is why you need to take great care of what you think and be aware of what kind of relationship you have with your thoughts.

The way to an increasing awareness of your thoughts is to pay attention to the way you feel. Not only will your feelings be the indicators of where you have let your thoughts go, but your external relationships will also always reflect what is going on in your thinking. This is because your powerful mind communicates all the time.

The mind is very powerful, and never loses its creative force. It never sleeps. Every instant it is creating. It is hard to recognize that thought and belief combine into a power surge that can literally move mountains.

We need to have experiences that show us that we are more than a body and that we can communicate beyond the body. Sometimes people will tell me they have a dream where they can fly and experience freedom. In whatever way is given to us, in whatever way we attract, we need to have an experience that we are more than a body. There is a lot of research around near-death experiences and out-of-body experiences and lots and lots of reports around people who are in comas and unconscious. If communication were based on the body and certain brain activity, a coma would seem like a definite break in communication. Yet over and over, we hear stories of patients who come out of comas and say things like, "Why did you tell that story about me?" This shows clearly that communication is not limited to the body. This shows that we can begin to loosen up from the idea that we are powerless and go beyond preconceived limits with our communication. Sometimes we can even have telepathic experiences. It works more like prayers: you send out a vibe with your thoughts, then the universe responds to that vibe, and that is reflected directly in the world around you. This is what I mean when I say that you communicate all the time.

The more we allow for open and transparent communication, the more we feel our expansiveness. Therefore, this is a very helpful prayer to the Holy Spirit: "Please show me how to use the body and communication best to expand my perception." This expanded perception gives us a feeling of a much stronger connection to everyone and everything.

Communing with Spirit in Communication

The Holy Spirit uses the body for only one purpose, and that is as a communication device to help the mind regain the awareness that true communication is through Spirit and that true communication is with the Creator. Because the mind has fallen asleep and believes in separation and bodies, the Spirit has to use what the separated mind believes in. For example, you go about your day using words as you speak and maybe as you write, so the Holy Spirit will guide you through words to train the mind to come back into true communion. The purpose of Spirit-inspired communication is to go beyond the interpersonal communication to communion with the One.

The more you practice this, the more you let Spirit pour through you and express through you. You don't hold back anymore. You start to have an experience of an inner dialogue, as if you are teaching yourself, as if there is nobody else in the universe but you. There is just one mind, but that one mind has been forgotten and seems to have fragmented off into billions of pieces that only know of the little personality self.

In everything you do, let your practice become to see the body and personality self as your means but never the "end goal." When the body and the person are the focus and are given too much attention, they become the end rather than means. Let your mind be the end, your divine mind, the mind that you truly are, the mind that thinks with God. The whole purpose of life is to have a connected experience. Let your intuition take charge. Your ego has been running the show for quite a while without getting to what you really, truly want. It has been striving—another goal, improving the body, another relationship—seeking and not finding. Now you can start allowing your mind to be the end and the body the means for this end in all your relationships and situations in life. You can start to see that your body has only one purpose: to be a communication device that the Spirit can use to expand your perception. Healing your mind deserves your full attention. If you let the body be your communication device and if you don't withhold any communication, everything channels into one experience.

In trusting and following the Holy Spirit, you are shown a sense of intimacy and connection that is not dependent on bodies being together. Why does it sometimes feel so terrible when the bodies go apart? Separation anxiety happens when you believe that there can be a break in communication. When you feel located in a body in a particular place in space, you can feel very, very alone.

EXERCISE: Feel Connected in Your Communication

When you are ready to begin your next assignment, take your usual few minutes to calm and quiet your mind. Take several deep breaths, remembering your healing purpose, and invite the Holy Spirit to be with you during this process. In this exercise, you are going to look at fear of communication. When you feel ready to look within, open your mind to the following steps:

1. Choose a current relationship where you are holding back from communicating. Write down all the ways you hold back.

2. Identify situations where you have opportunities to speak up, share, or connect and still feel you hold back. Write them down.

3. Are you willing to communicate how you really feel in order to experience true connection? Write down your immediate response. If you notice any resistance or hesitation, be honest about it and make notes.

4. Journal about the relationship: your thoughts, feelings, and beliefs about yourself and the other. Don't leave anything out of your exploration. Include thoughts about a specific situation if this comes to mind.

5. Write a list of all the things you would say to the person involved. For the purpose of the exercise, don't exclude anything out of a belief that you need to be nice or hold up a certain mask, for example.

6. Do you have any expectations about the other person's response? Write them down. What responses do you fear? What responses do you hope for?

7. Are you willing to let go of your expectations and open to a new perspective? Know that releasing your expectations is the means to peace. Take time to go into this inquiry and journal about your observations.

8. Open your mind to the light behind your perception of the other person and remember your healing purpose. Take a deep breath, welcome a prayerful state of mind, and relax. Ask the Spirit for guidance about what it is you are to do or say to them and finally, give this relationship over to Him.

Sharing Freely Is Loving

When you make it a priority to follow the Holy Spirit's inspiration in your heart and stay in full open communication with others and with God, doubt and fear will start to disappear and not be reflected by other people anymore. When you have integrity—when what you think, say, and do, are in alignment—you are at peace.

God created us in truth as love; therefore, this is the only thing that we can truly share. Words of wisdom pour through you when you are in communion with your Creator, whether that be with other people, through the Internet, or anything that blesses.

CHAPTER 13

COLLABORATION

Divine collaboration differs from special relationships in every way, as it holds the promise of a lived experience of relationship without expectations at its core. It has a deep respect and an understanding that transcends the usual roles we play. It wants nothing from another, but each person within a holy collaborative relationship is sharing something that is deeply nurturing, leaving each feeling full and grateful. These are the relationships that offer an experience of joining with something much greater.

Collaborative Assignments for Deeper Alignment with Spirit

Once you have made the decision to make healing the goal for your relationships, the Holy Spirit provides the means for it to happen. There is a divine plan available for our worldly interpersonal relationships, though this plan is generally hidden until our minds have reached a certain maturity. The purpose of a collaborative relationship, as well as of every assignment, is to learn as deeply as you can about who you truly are.

Healing through relationships comes in many forms. Some people don't feel intuitively guided or drawn in to an intimate or romantic relationship since they have plenty of relationships in their daily life, at work, and with friends and relatives. There are many different assignments that we can use to align with the Holy Spirit, and couple relationships can be major assignments. They are among the most potent training grounds in this world.

You need a sense of a shared purpose in relationship assignments, a commitment, that is always directed to the light and the healing. The unconscious mind is filled with much darkness that has to be exposed. You need to go through the darkness to arrive at the light. It can seem like a long, dark tunnel; sometimes you may wonder if there is light at the end. The shared purpose is what sustains you as you move through the darkness to reach the light.

It is not always immediately obvious how a relationship can be truly helpful. Sometimes two people are not even conscious of how important it is that they be together. The relationships or assignments can be very intense. If one or the other leaves the relationship, one should not worry; the lesson will come back. It will be repeated, maybe with another person. Because once readiness and willingness are in alignment, we attract the means for what we need to heal until it's healed. It's helpful to be aware that the ego, being scared of the end, does not like this, so it's going to fight against the means, against the relationships.

Relationships offer endless opportunities for collaboration. They serve as a backdrop to come together. Collaborative relationships with a healing purpose contain two qualities: they are undefined, and they are guided. Those qualities aren't typically part of relationships in this world.

The "undefined" part is very scary to the ego, but it is an essential entry point. Openness is one of the main doorways to a holy relationship and thus to freedom. An undefined relationship is about being willing to be open, to just show up. This is why collaborative relationships don't have the rigidity, the expectations, and the demands that linear (time-based) or special relationships have. When the relationship is undefined, there isn't a structure or an agenda already set in place. There isn't a standard that the relationship has to meet. There is no role to live up to. You don't ever have to put any thought into how to keep someone happy or how to keep the relationship alive. Imagine what that would be like.

The "guided" part is very important because this is how it can be used by the Holy Spirit for healing and the highest good. The relationship is for a higher purpose and doesn't have a form goal. In fact, you don't know what outcome is best or how to achieve it. So, it's essential to leave space for the Spirit to make it obvious. A collaborative relationship contains an inspiration and an agreement to be used together in some helpful way that benefits the healing of the mind and therefore blesses the whole universe.

Opposing the idea of collaborative assignments for healing, the ego basically says, "Distract yourself, use entertainment and fantasy, and forget about commitment to a mind-training practice or collaboration. Live it up because you're going to die anyway." The Holy Spirit is saying there is much more than that. When you reach a certain stage of maturity, you can be guided into shorter or longer assignments. You can even have lifelong relationships or partnerships where the teaching-learning balance is perfect. And, if you decide to learn it, the perfect lesson is laid before you and can be learned. This is very optimistic. Spiritually, two are drawn together because of this teaching-learning balance, and there will be countless opportunities to really get the lesson. It is worth hanging in there when that happens!

The Power of Joining

An experience of collaborative joining is an experience of being connected in mind. It's an experience of being deeply joined in a shared purpose: the healing and forgiveness of illusion. Being in collaborative relationship can be a bit like the 12-step programs, where you have a sponsor. A sponsor is a trusted brother or sister to join with on decisions, a joining that shows you the way or guides you. When you link up in mind with others to join in decision making, you are open to asking and to be shown the direction. You are not operating from a place of thinking you already know, where you believe you don't need to join or listen. Things that weren't clear before always become clear through joining and open communication. It's not that others necessarily know better than you. Nobody really knows. It is the joining that is so powerful and makes the direction clear. It's a different focus than just trying to accomplish things. After a while, the joining becomes internalized to a point where you become really humble as you just ease into a state of inner listening, flowing, and following.

In the ego's world, the personality and the personal perspective is the baseline for everything. It is sticky, it is enmeshed, and it is uncomfortable. There is an underlying low-level anxiety with it that can increase with different things you do. But your holy companions, your friends in this purpose, are showing up as symbols of love and support and saying, "Let's go on this journey together. Let's remember who we truly are. Let's be shown our wholeness. Let's not be tempted to become depressed." There is much more that awaits beyond the dismantling of the ego.

There is an immense sense of freedom that comes with vibrational connections and collaborations. Being connected to the Spirit, you feel free. You don't feel bound to the world. Your mind is not thinking, *How am I going to survive, what's going to happen tomorrow, and how am I going to deal with this and that?*, the typical things that the egoic mind is focusing on. In holy collaboration, your mind is lifted into a realm that's higher than those doubts, fears, and concerns, and your spirit emanates from this higher place. It's divine!

EXERCISE: Clearing the Way for Collaboration

Sit quietly and allow a current relationship to come into awareness. Any relationship that comes to your mind can be used. You can repeat this exercise as many times as you'd like and with any of your relationships. Use your journal to answer the following questions.

1. How do you define the role you play in the relationship? Examples could be girlfriend, husband, friend, mother, grandparent, or boss. Include what expectations you have of yourself in that role.

2. How important is it that you define yourself as this role? Write down any thoughts that cross your mind, such as *It is my identity. I would be lost without this. I worked hard to get to here. I have proven myself worthy of it. Others depend on me to uphold them.*

3. What roles have you assigned the other person in this relationship, and what are your expectations of them? For example, *I*

expect my husband to provide for me and my family and love me as his wife. I expect my sister to be supportive and always agree with me.

4. Is there a link between the different roles you have assigned for both of you and the expectations you have about the relationship? Describe it in your journal.

5. Finally, in your definition of the relationship (marriage, friendship, coworker, or another agreement), ask yourself: How does this definition lock you and the other into place? Write down how you feel about this.

6. Does this definition of the relationship adhere to social or cultural standards and past thinking? Write down what those standards are and your thoughts and associations around them.

Put away your pen now and gently imagine yourself in this same relationship but without the expectations you have identified. Let any feelings you may have about releasing the relationship as you currently see it come to the surface. Take your time to allow this to feel helpful and relaxing.

Now it's time to make a promise or prayer for healing:

Holy Spirit, help me to expand my view of this relationship so that I may realize our shared nature of innocence, peace, and love. Show me even in small ways that You provide the miracle I'm seeking in all my relationships. Guide me so that I may be truly happy.

Amen.

It only takes a little willingness, so I encourage you to envision your relationship outside of past parameters and into purpose. Allow an experience of giving over your relationship for the purpose of healing. You may feel some uneasiness or discomfort when looking at changing old habits of relating with others. The greatest shift that I encourage you to make is the one in your mind. Allow yourself to change the direction of your thinking, and this will be reflected in your relationships.

A Collaborative Purpose

There may be many in your circle of relationships who are not able to hear about your desire for deepening and healing. The important thing is to allow yourself to look at these concerns and allow the fear to rise from within to be released. Remember that all of your concerns or discomforts come from the ego's fear of love. So, having this broader context for moving ahead with the suggestions I have offered can make the process easier to give yourself allowance for imperfection and fears that arise. Allow the excitement of the journey and the tickle in your heart for healing to guide the way.

The more you practice showing up with the purpose of the Holy Spirit in the forefront, the more you start to draw forth witnesses of this new purpose. Relationships and collaboration may take on a whole new meaning! It can be with old friends who are ready to expand with you or new ones coming into your life as reflections of your new purpose. It really only takes practice. It doesn't matter how long you've been on the spiritual journey; it's about your willingness to practice the steps, to practice the principles, and to invite and allow the healing collaborations.

It is not necessary that you fully believe in or welcome these practices. It is their use that will show you they are true. That's powerful. That's a huge emphasis on practical application. Don't be disheartened if you find yourself resisting the unconditional love impulse as it arises in these "new" relationships. The ego is extremely threatened by this impulse for unconditional love, for agape love. Be assured, as you align with the purpose of love and joy, a flood of miracles will show up and naturally dissolve all the unhelpful thoughts and fears.

CHAPTER 14

HOLY RELATIONSHIP

Finding yourself on Earth comes with the belief that you could leave God and exist in a far, far land that's very strange and very different than Home. You may feel at times like you are caught in no-mans-land. You are just in between, you're in betwixt in this transformation, and it does not feel stable. It doesn't feel consistent. It doesn't feel harmonious. It feels stirred up, like there's a great sorting out going on, and you are smack-dab in the middle of the sorting. That's when you're grateful to have a companion or a partner, and you can say, "Here we go; another day of this healing process. Let's commit to purpose, and we'll be ready for whatever is coming our way!"

As you make a stronger commitment to healing your mind and if you have a relationship with a special partner, you may feel your relationship begin to transform and shift as you align and open to the Spirit's path. The relationship is basically leaving its former goal, maybe of gratification, for a higher goal of peace of mind. This is an experience of relationships becoming less personal and more encompassing. In other words, the move from special relationship to holy relationship is directly related to the shift from a special—distinct and separate—purpose to a holy purpose in your mind. The decision for holiness or holy relationship comes from within and is reflected as a deeply felt purpose in each and every encounter and situation. Entering into holy relationship means that you will find a deeper meaning in the stillness of your mind. You will be happy because you experience the meaning of the present moment and the miracle that is your essence. This is the birth and the being of your Self.

Until you reach this higher self-realization, people in your life are just concretized beliefs, acting out the unhealed parts of your mind. At times it can look very dysfunctional, with lots of hiding and people pleasing. This is why you need supportive friends and holy companions. As you move forward, after a lot of inner work and clearing, you move toward holy relationship. From there you will begin to draw forth more and more witnesses to your healed mind and to the growing love in your heart. You will attract vibrational connections.

Imagine partnering with someone or a group of people who, after you pour your heart out, simply say, "What do you want?" Imagine if you asked for help or advice, and they simply focused you back to the desire of your heart rather than giving you their opinions on what you should do. This is the same as saying, "I love you. I love you. I totally, unconditionally love you. Now, what do you want? I loved you before your decision and I will love you after your decision." It's really a beautiful expression of love when you have the strength and confidence to allow someone to make a decision and love them beyond whatever that decision is. These relationships are the beginning of the undoing of linear, special relationships. They are healing because of their purpose. Your inner calling for holy relationship will bring your whole life in alignment with this purpose. This is my invitation to everyone: let us join together in a very trusting relationship so we may hear the answers that are freely given to us by the Holy Spirit.

Inviting the Holy Spirit into Relationships

A holy relationship is born out of the release of the layers of darkness below the surface of our awareness. The fastest way to transform a special relationship into a holy relationship and wake up to a happy dream is a combination of silence and committed relationship.

Silence is found through short or extended times of contemplation and prayer or meditation, quiet times where you are able to go deep within and expand in Spirit and look at your thoughts and beliefs. Combined with a committed relationship, devoted to forgiveness and communication, this is the fast track to peace of mind and to enlightenment. It is a quick, powerful, supportive, and at times, intense way through the darkness to the light within. It is very helpful to remember that it doesn't really matter what forgiveness and healing look like in form; it is more about what you want the relationship to be for, what purpose you give to the relationship. When the relationship is given over to serve the Holy Spirit's purpose rather than the ego's, the healing can be very rapid. Holy relationship is a means to save time for yourself and the whole universe.

The transition from specialness to holiness will result in a gradual dismantling of the ego that comes from your choice for peace—choosing this present moment over specialness. It is about self-honesty. It is always very helpful to take time to pause and remember the purpose of a relationship. When your mind is ready, you will inevitably invite the Holy Spirit to come into the relationship. Once the Holy Spirit enters, it can temporarily become very intense. This is because inviting the Holy Spirit is asking for a purification to occur, to align the relationship with true love. The reason why the relationship can become more intense is because the ego does not like the new purpose. The ego gave the relationship the old purpose of personal gratification, dependency, or getting something from the other, which it wants to use to maintain itself. When you invite the Holy Spirit, you unplug from everything that is not true love, and if the relationship has deeply rooted habits not aligned with Spirit's purpose, then the whole foundation for the relationship will start to teeter and shake. This is an important phase of maintaining trust. You have to allow the Holy Spirit to do the work even though you may be tempted to give up. It's helpful at this time to be in touch with your feelings and be willing to talk about them. When you shift from attack to love, love is extended and comes back to you. It just takes willingness to practice. Don't let the ego dissuade you.

All relationships, even the ones where hatred has entered, can and will turn into holy or sacred relationships when you give them over to the Holy Spirit. It is only in that giving that you share the same purpose and truly have a relationship. From that point on, your alignment with Spirit will create a space for open communication and a nonjudgmental, safe place where you will stop hiding and protecting feelings. You will have honest communication; a deeper way of communicating that will become more and more consistent.

Seeing the Truth of Christ in Each Other

Recurring difficulties, perhaps grievances or agendas, or a feeling of fear or tightness around a person happens because you have forgotten the truth about them, and you have also forgotten the truth about yourself. When you are interacting with a brother or when you are speaking to a sister, remember that what you say is what you yourself most need to hear. Are you gentle when you speak with your brother or sister because you see the truth in them? It's not so much even the words; you want the love and gentleness of the Spirit. This is what you can offer to every brother you meet and every sister you think of.

> Christ is God's Son as He created Him. He is the Self we share, uniting us with one another, and with God as well. He is the Thought which still abides within the Mind that is His Source. He has not left His holy home, nor lost the innocence in which He was created. He abides unchanged forever in the Mind of God.

Mother Teresa taught this. She told her devotees to see the face of Christ in everyone they look upon. When I heard that, I thought, *She's teaching holy relationship.* She made it clear that was their only purpose. She believed that holy relationship is a total commitment, moment to moment. She taught holy relationship through healed perception and through service. It wasn't about the behaviors; it was about seeing the face of Christ in every single person they met and following the guidance of the Spirit.

You can also see holy relationship as a relationship between you and the Holy Spirit. The point of authentic spirituality, of holy relationship, is to discover the now and the eternal and the power of the present moment that is the gateway to eternity. Therefore, holy relationship is not in a specific form, and so you will not arrive at some point in time where you look around in the world and say, "By golly, I finally reached my holy relationship, and it looks like I expected." Instead, it is a glorious state of mind, a state of nonjudgment. Imagine how still your mind would be if you were in a state of complete rest where you perceive your partner and everyone else from a place of complete nonjudgment, where you didn't have one single opinion about them. This alignment and understanding within the relationship leads to a powerful connection and to an experience of holiness.

EXERCISE: Uncover the Miracles in Relationships

To listen to a recorded version of this exercise and the prayer, go to http://www.newharbinger.com/41870.

There is a tremendous release and deep peace that comes from meeting yourself and your brothers totally without judgment. A miracle exists in every relationship, in every moment. To reveal the miracle, you must eliminate the obstacle hiding it. This obstacle, which stands between you and others, is a gap caused by a lack of communication, with other people or with the Holy Spirit. It is formed from judgments, grievances, blame, hurt, anger, and all other ego-serving emotions. It is ultimately formed by the belief in separation. You are the only one who reinforces the ego's ability to separate you from others when you engage and maintain grievances. Doing this two-part exercise with attention and willingness has the potential to remove this obstacle, which was erected by the ego, and release you, your relationship, and everyone from darkness to reveal the light of the miracle.

You will practice seeing this obstacle as a call for love. This is how you see it with the Holy Spirit.

Part 1. Praying for a Unified Perception

Give yourself plenty of time to quietly go inward with this prayer. You can read it aloud, pause to contemplate it, copy it into your journal, or post it on your refrigerator as a reminder. You may repeat this prayer as often as you want to really focus your attention on your desire to have an experience of union. Pray for an experience of these words.

My brother and sister and I are the same.

I am grateful to have them as a mirror

to see the unhealed thoughts in my mind.

I desire to see past all differences,

to the truth of who we are.

This prayer can give you a glimpse into the nature of the miracle and the transformative shift in the mind from specialness to holiness. There will be no question of the beauty and validity of this fresh and new experience. You are opening to the miracle of releasing the other and yourself from specialness and realizing your identity is far beyond the ego and far more expansive than the thoughts that held you back.

Part 2. Contemplating Union

You may now hear the call for love in yourself or your partner and feel a softening within. Open to the mind's call for love. When you bring your irritations to the light of love, your relationship becomes a path to healing.

Bring a relationship to mind and spend a few minutes writing in your journal any differences you are aware of between yourself and the other person. Become aware that there is a perceived split or a gap. Now, get comfortable, take some deep breaths, and reflect on the following:

"Where two or more are gathered, there I AM." Where we are gathered with someone in purpose, the Spirit's presence is with us. In this recognition, all personal concepts are undone, such as competition, success, reciprocity, personal gain, and pride. The aim of a holy relationship is to let go of any sense of individual interests for the benefit of the whole, the one mind.

For this part of the exercise, I'd like you to be willing to see, if only for a moment, your and your partner's goal as the same goal, that there is no difference. Go within and allow your mind to sink beyond distracting thoughts to reach a clean space that is filled with light to welcome this idea. Take as much time as you need to contemplate and experience the meaning of this profound idea.

"Even at the level of the most casual encounter it is possible for two people to lose sight of separate interests if only for a moment. That moment will be enough. Salvation has come."

Seeing you and your partner as innocent, with the same core purpose, is to see past all seeming differences. The way is to move beyond all concepts of attack, defense, and separate interests to the bliss and joy of this freedom, and to come wholly empty handed unto God.

A Mechanism for Miracles

Being in holy relationship is to be fully present with no thoughts of the past intruding. It's very free-flowing and open, free of expectations and limits, and free of the egoic motive to get something. Therefore, it is free of the belief in reciprocity. There's a sense of respect with holy relationship, a sense of trust. You don't have to have a special role or be in a Buddhist monastery to allow for a holy relationship. It's an elevation of purpose in the mind, and this can happen anywhere and with anyone. It can be experienced in a brief encounter at the supermarket or in an extended relationship with family or a friend.

The essence of a holy relationship is an experience of a joining that includes full and open communication where nothing is hidden. Open communication turns relationships into a wonderful mechanism to inspire, to bless, and to help us remember the truth of who we really are. This is the most glorious experience. The ego made bodies and interpersonal relationships as a substitute for total, open communication. As a result, we have fear-based egoic relationships based upon lack and scarcity, which don't lead to truth. So, when we return to open communication, it is like communion, like a telepathic awareness of love, like a happy dance. And so holy relationship is a symbol used only to reflect the divinity of God's love.

When you give over the situations and relationships in your life to the Holy Spirit and allow Him to use you for a holy purpose, there is a great sense of fulfillment. In your intimate relationships and daily encounters, the best thing you can do is pause, and then ask the questions, "What is this for? How can this relationship or encounter raise my mind higher?" You can pray, "Am I willing to give this relationship or encounter over to You now, God? Please show me how I can do that." Use this prayer to get in touch with your true feelings and learn to be transparent with the one in front of you. And, learn to listen! Then every single relationship becomes an opportunity to extend and a way to fulfill your function. That is going to make the relationship extremely fulfilling and very purposeful, and this is miraculous!

PART IV

BEING THE MIRACLE

CHAPTER 15

HEALING

All forms of sickness, without exception, have their origin in the idea that we could be separate from our Source. This is the original attack thought. But truly, our Source could not possibly create sickness. Would all the glory of the Kingdom of Heaven or nirvana, just say, "Oh yeah, let's throw in a little sickness into the mix? It's perfect as it is, but let's give it a little contrast!" It would not and could not do that. I think most people on a deep level sense that there is some kind of trick going on with sickness. This chapter will show how, when you start to tune in to that intuitive knowledge and realize the power of your mind, to see that you have the capacity within: the power inside to heal, to be healthy and well, and to be peaceful, joyful, and happy. The experience of sickness in the body then can be your strong call and incentive to go inside and to, with the help of the Holy Spirit, see things differently.

True Healing Equals Peace of Mind

Because everything is consciousness, everything we see and experience is only really happening in the mind. It can be surprising at first, even shocking, but what we call physical symptoms in the body are actually thoughts in the mind. In other words, like the whole world, our body is just a projection. This brings us to the natural conclusion that everything around sickness—symptoms, different diseases, pain, and suffering—is nothing more than a projection of the mind.

We are getting more and more clues and hints that things are not what they seem, including within the field of medicine. There are numerous research studies about the power of the mind over matter, and the power of faith, prayer, and belief. Doctors are prescribing placebos and achieving results. All of this breaks away from the idea that anything in form has a causative effect on the body. It's pointing us back to the power of the mind.

When we get into looking at our thoughts, we start to uncover that there are certain thought patterns and beliefs that aren't conducive to our peace of mind. We discover that we don't feel well when we complain and hold judgments. When we look deeper, we discover that it is the judgmental thought patterns that are the actual cause of symptoms and sickness.

We can become disillusioned when healing does not occur. This is because we have identified the problem in form rather than in our thinking—our only focus is to fix symptoms, change conditions of the body, or change something in our environment. But sickness does not come from germs or viruses. Sickness does not come from things in the world. Sickness is a projection of our attack thoughts. We first project our attack thoughts onto the body; then we give the effect of these attack thoughts a name, like cancer or the flu.

If you look to the body or the world for the cause of sickness or its solution, you will be trying to solve what is actually a conflict in the mind through changing external circumstances. And this is the grand deception. When you realize that external circumstances do not provide a lasting solution, you will make a switch and say, "I'm not going to play this game anymore! I'm going to stop looking for causes of sickness in the world and in the body." Sometimes we go through the school of hard knocks before we are ready to hear that we have to look inside. We can't just say, "Well, one option is to look inside." It's absolutely crucial for our peace of mind and well-being that we look inside. There is no other way to heal. There isn't even an external "God" to pray to that can fix it for you. Instead of trying to pray to "Papa" in the sky and hoping he's listening—which is kind of what's been going on for millennia—we need go far beyond the hopes and attempts of asking the man with the white beard on the clouds, an external God, for healing. Instead, when we want to heal, we need to go very deep into the mind to release the original attack thought. This is the only way to healing!

People who have heard me say that sickness is a decision think it's bizarre that anyone in their right mind would choose to be sick. And that's correct. No one in their right mind would choose to be sick!" Sickness is just a wrong-minded decision. And so, obviously, this decision has to get exposed and released. The metaphysics behind sickness can be explained this way: Because we believe we have pulled away and separated from God and our home in Heaven, we believe that there could be some punishment or retribution, or some price to pay. This fear of retribution from God is unconscious. Because of this and of being unaware of the truth that you can be hurt by nothing but your thoughts, the mind is actually afraid of healing, and this is why it makes itself sick. It is saying: "The body is real; it is my identity." This fear strengthens our belief in the body as our identity rather than the mind.

The perceptual world is the outer ring of the levels of the mind (as shown in the illustration in chapter 2). This is where we find our perception of sickness. If we perceive a symptom, a painful toe for example, and we spend lots of money, effort, and resources addressing this toe—there may have been a huge focus for years on this toe—we are looking in the wrong place for healing. We are looking to the external perceptual realm. What we really need to do, first of all, is to take the focus off the toe. The toe and the pain in the toe is an *effect*. The mind is misdirected when it's so riveted on what's just an effect. We have to pull the attention off the toe and open to the awareness that the problem does not have anything to do with the specifics—the pain or the toe. The problem is a perceptual problem. We may need a lot of convincing to realize this, and we will have to remind ourselves over and over and train our mind to pull our attention off of effects. We do this by stepping away from our current perception and training our mind to find and realize the real cause of our problems: the belief in separation. This is the only real and lasting option for relief. It's reframing the problem from perception and pulling it back to see that it's much more profound than that. The toe is just a tiny effect of the actual problem.

Sickness Is a Grievance

Sickness, in other words, is wrong-minded thinking. It is a grievance, and only forgiveness heals a grievance. This grievance lies much, much deeper than the surface symptoms that you are aware of. In fact, the grievance probably doesn't even seem to have any overt or obvious connection to the symptom. You may not understand it consciously, but you will begin to feel an impetus to go much, much deeper and start to welcome what's unconscious into awareness. And this is really a time of rejoicing. It's not a time of thinking you have failed to find a solution to this specific symptom. It's more like a time of rejoicing that you're getting to the point where you want to look much deeper inside. So rather than looking for symptom relief, you start to look for perceptual problem relief. It is a huge difference! It's a relief to no longer try to heal the toe, but rather to focus on the unconscious wrong-minded thinking that has projected the painful toe: the story of how it happened, the life situation in general, the body, and the whole universe.

We can see sickness as a call for help. It is a call for love. By exercising our willingness to expose and dispel our attack thoughts, we can answer this call for help and experience healing—physically, emotionally, and mentally. We start to clearly see that the ego is constantly trying to play a major trick on us by covering the original attack thought of separation with other surface attack thoughts that generate the sickness: attack thoughts around the body, attack thoughts around the toe, fear thoughts around any symptom that you seem to have.

It can take a lot of convincing to accept that all illness is actually mental illness, that it is all in the mind. The convincing will happen through miracles that will help us fully release the belief that events and circumstances are the cause of sickness.

Feeling sick is a call for us to question our unconscious beliefs and conclusions and to gently invite another perception. We do this step by step, little by little, practicing with what's currently in front of us in our awareness, in our life.

If somebody says they are ill, the immediate thoughts that follow are usually questions about what is wrong with them, what is hurting them, what are the symptoms, and what is the diagnosis. There is such a focus and fixation on the body and physical symptoms, on the particulars of the disease, and the form of the illness. The world has set up a sophisticated medical model to treat and prevent physical and mental health problems. As such, there is often a desire to try to find the answers on the level of form. The attempts at solutions are endless: diet, exercise, surgery, and a countless variety of different therapies and practices.

Dismantle and Heal

Let's take a look at a scenario that could have a transcending nature for you if you yearn for healing. A patient typically goes to a doctor or therapist because they want a magical shift. They want a better life in form. They want the doctor to magically take away their problems, their difficulties, and their pains and symptoms. And herein lies the problem. Getting a better life in form is just a temporary shift; it can never be lasting. The true healer, the Holy Spirit, is the real therapist and doctor. However, the patient thinks twice about accepting this healing, since healing with the Holy Spirit requires a complete shift. It means that they would have their self-concept, their entire world, dismantled. They might think, *I didn't ask you to take my life away. I asked you to make it better! Give me a better life; give me a better illusion instead of the dismantling.* Because of the fear of the loss of this life as they know it, the patient will not trust the Holy Spirit, so the sickness and the temporary fixes churn on and on like a treadmill.

But dismantling is what we are in for now. When we go for healing, we are in for a journey of letting go of everything we believe and everything we think we know, and this is how we discover the full power and potential of our holy mind. Healing occurs the instant we no longer see any value in sickness. It can be hard to understand what that even means! First we have to admit that we must have some kind of attraction to sickness—a sick attraction to wrong-mindedness, a sick attraction to pain, a sick attraction to guilt, or an addiction to misery. People who have gone through a 12-steps program often feel that they had some kind of sick attraction to their addictions. And what we need to acknowledge is that deep down, we are choosing our sickness. It comes from a bad thinking habit. But you can change your habit. Whatever you made can be unmade. Whatever you thought you did can be undone. No matter how bad you think it has become, it is reversible because you can accept the correction in your mind. You just need to quit hiding. You must go inside, face what's there, and forgive it.

We are responsible for what we think, and if we hold on to ego thoughts, fear will inevitably be the emotion that we experience. There is usually a resistance to completely letting go of these thoughts because many of them are part of a defense mechanism that the mind uses to try to keep things the way they are. We have to be convinced through miracles that it is safe to let go of our habitual thinking—the judgments and the attack thoughts—and trust that this is the only way we can heal our mind. We are invited to join with the Holy Spirit to have our unconscious issues flushed into awareness so we can transcend them completely. When we rise above the battleground of our conflicts and hurts, peace starts to settle in our mind. Then there's no longer a need to act out the grievances and wrong-minded thinking in the form of sickness.

Free from Grievances

There can be an enormous temptation to be hard on yourself as you go through your healing process. Don't give in to it. The ego wants to sabotage the whole healing process by having you throw in the towel, thinking it's too difficult. Maybe you think you're not doing it good enough or that you'll never get past the obstacles, the sickness, or the darkness of your wrong-minded thinking. The ego just wants you to come up with some conclusion to shut down your willingness. But it is a fact that the ego has no defense when your willingness is joined with the Holy Spirit. This ignites a huge powerful healing. The only thing that you are really asked to do is offer your willingness, and if you stay willing, it can be a pretty quick journey!

Here is a story that clearly shows how a little willingness to forgive can bring about a powerful healing. I used to work at a hospice. One day I went for lunch with a colleague, who is also a minister, as he wanted to talk. He looked at me and said, "I have been diagnosed with leukemia, and it's pretty far advanced, so I don't know how many more weeks I can continue on with the hospice training."

I looked at him, and the Holy Spirit guided me to say, "Is there somebody in your life who used to be really close to you, someone whom you used to just talk and laugh with, but whom you haven't spoken to in years?"

He sat back, he put his burger down, and he said, "How did you know about my sister?"

I said, "So, you haven't spoken to your sister in years?" And the Holy Spirit guided me to continue, "You know what, this leukemia diagnosis that you have got; it's not what you think it is. You have got a grievance against your sister, and you need to go home. Here is your hospice homework for the night: you need to go home and bury the hatchet; you need to call her and talk to her from your heart because I know that underneath the grievance, you love her."

And he said, "Yes...you're right; it is crazy; it is just absolutely crazy that I haven't spoken with her, that I have been carrying this for so long." Until then, he had not made the connection between the grievance with his sister and the leukemia. When I saw him a few weeks later, he told me that he had immediately contacted his sister and cleared the grievance. And when he later went in to the hospital, they couldn't find a trace of leukemia. It was all healed because he had gone through that opening of his heart. He buried the hatchet. He let go of the long-standing grievance. He shared with me that what he had been holding on to was so silly in hindsight.

This is what we can do now. We can allow ourselves to make the connections in our mind like, *Wow, it's important for me to be free of grievances so that I can heal.* And know, that with the help of the Holy Spirit, it *is* possible! Being free of grievances means that anyone from your entire life could show up; you could just sit there, look them in the eye, and smile; you could give them a big long hug; and you could love them without any sense of animosity, any belief in wrongdoing, not even any sense of irritation or annoyance.

When you remember who you are, you will bless everyone and everything you see. There will be no past and therefore no enemies. And you will look with love on all that you failed to see before.

You were just mistaken when you perceived that your brother or your sister wanted to attack or hurt you. It was you who wanted to throw something that was wounded in yourself onto them. Letting go of grievances and grudges is your most practical remedy. It is a miracle!

EXERCISE: Open Up to Healing

For this two-part exercise, find a quiet place where you will not be disturbed and have your journal with you. Turn your attention inward. See this as a devotional time that you set aside for yourself.

Part 1. Identifying and Releasing Your Grievances

In this exercise, you are going to look at the purpose a current upset or frustration seems to serve. Be very open to recognizing any "reasons" that you may be using to maintain sickness or a symptom. Allow yourself to settle inward; ask the Holy Spirit to help you see any thoughts and beliefs that are under the surface of your consciousness. Even if they are intense, just allow them. Your healing is worth the effort you put into your practice now. It will open your mind to the miracle of this present moment where all answers are given. You are going inside to heal.

In your journal, prayerfully write down your answers to the following:

1. List and describe a current disturbance, annoyance, or upset. It can be an irritation, a discomfort, or a physical symptom. Ask yourself: Is there someone or something I'm upset with? Who and what is it? Welcome and allow the feelings.

2. What might you be trying to "prove" to yourself or someone else by having these disturbances or symptoms? This may not

be apparent at first. Take your time and ask Spirit to help you see deeply into your mind.

3. Irritation or sickness of any kind comes with a feeling of separateness and withdrawal. Why are you choosing to be separate? List every possible reason. Make sure to not avoid anything.

The ego uses all disturbances and all forms of sickness to have you "prove" to yourself that you are limited, weak, and vulnerable. It can also use an illness to "prove" that you are vulnerable in order to receive attention and love from others. You may be using a grievance to avoid a particular event, situation, or person and "prove" that you are weak.

Take a moment with this prayer:

Holy Spirit, I trust You to show me what I need to see so that I can heal. Please help me see my thoughts so they may be released into Your loving hands. I seem to have grievances and symptoms; I seem to have things going on in my body. I open my mind to You now and ask You to show me that I am not upset, worried, or fearful for the reason I think.

Sit quietly. Notice how you are feeling. You may feel a sense of relief or anticipation, or you may notice feelings of discomfort. It's okay. Take your time. When you are ready, take the next step.

Now, invite these powerful, true ideas into your mind. Say to yourself:

There is no problem that is separate or apart from my mind. There is no problem that is separate or apart from my thoughts. I am willing to be wrong about my thoughts. I give them now to You, Holy Spirit. I want to heal. I want to be happy. I want to know love.

Part 2. Meditation: Going Beyond Grievances, Praying for Healing

Through your willingness to see your grievances as wrong-minded thoughts, you have risen above the battleground. True healing comes when you see that you have false beliefs about sickness and false beliefs about your identity. As you welcome and remember the truth, the fog that obscured the light of peace dissolves. I invite you to stay open and listen. Listen to the silence of your mind.

Imagine now that you are entering a space inside your mind where you can be totally relaxed and feel perfectly safe. Let go of any distractions, worries, or problems that may be calling for your attention. You can return to them later, if you wish. Take a few deep breaths and spend a few moments in quietness with this prayer.

Here, in this moment I give myself permission

to sink deep down to a place of rest inside my mind.

I come now into a safe, sacred space,

where my mind is open to the truth,

I offer You all of my doubts and call upon Your certainty.

I see that sickness and grievances are my calls for love.

I will no longer hide my nightmares from You;

I expose them. I release them.

I bring the darkness to Your light.

Now I am quiet,

in the midst of all the raspy noises of the world.

I sink down into deep stillness.

Today I look straight at every image or symptom,

realizing that the goal is inevitable;

the goal of love, happiness, joy, and peace.

Perfect love casts out all fear!

Today I trust the Holy Spirit…and I accept His trust in me.

I look within and find peace.

Amen.

Healing Yourself Is Healing the Universe

If you pray for healing but stay concerned with and look for symptoms, you need to redirect your mind, otherwise healing cannot occur. It will take a great deal of vigilance to bring your attention back to your mind and release all worry and concern around symptoms to the Holy Spirit. It takes determination to watch the doubt and fear thoughts and to keep handing them over. If the fear becomes too great, you may feel that going to the doctor or getting some medicine will support you temporarily while sincerely working with and looking at all of your thoughts and situations calling for forgiveness. This is okay because a fearful mind is itself a block to healing, to the awareness of love's presence. The feeling of trust arises naturally with a relaxed and grateful mind. Come into the prayer of your heart, be willing to have a change of perception, and feel the joy of healing! You are worthy of experiencing your real purpose, the only way to real and lasting healing.

It is important to see that there is an obvious choice. There are numerous opportunities to take the bait and perceive yourself as being separate, attacked, rejected, and abandoned. The ego has been sponsoring this attack and defense game for so long, and now you're going to shift and open to healing. This is a great shift of mind. When you begin to see your sickness as a call for love, you'll notice a softening, a change both in your mind and in your day-to-day life. And as you allow the love that you perceive as missing to be extended, you receive it immediately. It will get reflected right back to you as a miracle. This is how healing of the mind and the body works. Exactly as it is with mental healing, physical healing can always only be of the mind. When the mind has full and open communication and all wrong-minded thoughts have been raised to the light, healing will follow. The body will be a healthy tool or vehicle for a mind that is happy and at peace.

It's important to remember that when you genuinely desire healing for yourself or for others, your focus is not on whether the symptoms stay or disappear. The key is to not be invested in a bodily outcome or appearances. Remember that healing is not really about removal of symptoms; it is about returning your mind to God. Joining your mind with God,

your Source, will give complete clarity and awareness of your true identity. When you experience this, when you are fully present in the miracle
moment, you will have no perception of sickness, only unending peace,
a peace beyond understanding.

It is in coming back to inspiration and vibrancy that you heal. You
do this through holding the hand of the Holy Spirit in every moment.
Whether you want healing for an ailment, to heal tiredness to become
alert and vibrant, or just to have an inspiring day, this is always so. This
is your function of forgiveness in this world, and it will bring many miracles that transform your entire life. Bring it into your daily thinking and
daily decision making, moment to moment. This is the way to release the
ego. When you do not want to protect your ego, you are harmless. When
you are harmless, you cannot hurt anyone or yourself, neither your mind
nor your body.

Because you are working with your perception, others will heal as
you forgive and heal. It's exciting because it's an invitation from the Holy
Spirit to a whole new way of living. When you look at the tools you have
and the people in your life, you can make wise and helpful choices that
value the love that's in your heart. You will value your opening heart,
expanding and unfolding. And you will want to surround yourself with
everything that is conducive to your healing.

CHAPTER 16

FORGIVENESS

The ego has a version of forgiveness that humanity has bought hook, line, and sinker. The belief is "I forgive you for what you did to me, or I forgive myself for what I did to you." This is not really forgiveness. It doesn't work. It is no wonder that, in the Bible, Jesus was quoted as saying, "When you forgive, forgive seventy times seven." If you are forgiving in an ego way, you have to do it more than 490 times. It is endless. You could do it 490,000 times or 490 million times. If you just keep forgiving in the ego's way, you will still feel guilty, and you will wonder why it didn't work. I did it plenty of times. My gosh, how many Hail Marys do you have to do to get out of this difficult feeling? As long as you are trying to forgive what you believe somebody did to you or what you did to somebody, you will not really forgive. You are on the ego's playing field: it loves it when you get angry at something in the world. The ego is like a little spider sitting back in its web, saying, "Ha-ha, fooled them again. They think it is about this or that."

The ego is hiding behind the projection. It is disguised by what you project. You don't recognize that it is in charge. The ego's form of forgiveness makes an error real first, and then, out of your own goodness, you can forgive it. This way, you are attempting a forgiveness that can never accomplish the goal of peace.

The ego is the first premise of an erroneous thought system, and anyone who studies logic knows that if your first premise is faulty, then everything after it is faulty. True forgiveness is not like forgiveness of the world where you forgive somebody for what they did to you. Divine logic starts with another premise: you are whole; you are complete; you are innocent.

This leads to a way of forgiveness that truly works. It involves bringing the projections back in and taking full responsibility for your mind and thoughts. You forgive your *perception*, your idea of what you thought the other did, because *in truth* they did not do it. It was only a projection of belief. This may sound strange; the ego scratches its head and says, "Oh, forgiving what they didn't do, that sounds quite difficult." But your mind is powerful and made up everything you perceive. Complete forgiveness means seeing and deeply experiencing that *nothing happened*. This is peace of mind, the highest state.

The step we take in forgiveness now is about allowing perceptions and beliefs to come up in awareness and be released to the Spirit within. The way is to join with others, rather than separating from them, and *being* the forgiveness. Being the forgiveness takes blame off the objects: forgiving my mother, forgiving my father, forgiving the Holocaust, forgiving white supremacy, forgiving racism, forgiving the president, forgiving my body. When you take the focus off all the specific things that blame seems to be about and take it all the way in, you will realize you are only forgiving the self that you thought you made, the self that took the place of what you truly are.

As I got into mysticism, I seemed to fail in the role and image of a son. At one point, my father came to me with a look of remorse in his eyes, a look of such sadness. These words came out of his mouth, "Dave, I wasn't a very good father." It was a moment of admission. I had already reached a consistent experience of peace at that point, and I said, "That is nonsense. You did the best you could do, based on what you believed. And I did the best I could do, based on what I believed." Whatever that was—autopilot, repression, projection—at the time, it was the best I could do, based on what I believed about myself. I said, "This game is over now. I'm not going to ever hold you to anything. I'm not going to hold you to the dad role, and I'm not holding me to the son role because I have seen that the ego made up those roles."

God creates us as Spirit, not as mothers, fathers, sisters, and brothers. When I let go of playing these roles, my relationships lit up. I had forgiven the belief in roles. My father and I had the happiest and most loving, joyful relationship, and that relationship continued until the day that he passed away. At our last encounter, we were not holding onto the past; we were rejoicing in truth, joy, and happiness!

The Cause of Any Problem—and the Solution

An unforgiving mind experiences guilt and suffering. It experiences differences. The cause of any and all the problems you can think of is basically just an unforgiving mind, while a forgiving mind brings everything you want. It brings contentment, peace, and a deep sense of connection. The solution to anything is forgiveness, forgiveness of what is not true. What is not true is everything that is not love. This includes all the judgments that we see and think about the world, about ourselves, and about others.

Out of all the concepts believed in this world, forgiveness is the only truly helpful one.

Dream softly of your sinless brother who unites with you in holy innocence. Dream of your brother's kindnesses instead of dwelling in your dreams on his mistakes. Select his thoughtfulness to dream about instead of counting up the hurts he gave. Forgive him his illusions, and give thanks to him for all the helpfulness he gave. And do not brush aside his many gifts because he is not perfect in your dreams.

Brother, come and let me look on you. Your loveliness reflects my own. Your sinlessness is mine. You stand forgiven, and I stand with you.

It is a miracle to let go of grievances by allowing memories and beliefs to surface in awareness and then letting them go. This is how you forgive: When the temptation to perceive yourself as unfairly treated arises, surrender the thought, the perspective, and the desire to be "right" about the way it was "set up" or seemed to be, let go into the miracle. As this becomes a habit, being a miracle worker is happily discovered as our function in all situations! We are joined in the purpose of forgiveness, and I am grateful this is so.

When I was working with my own healing over the years, I finally got to the point where I turned the tables. I began to allow myself to feel the darkness and emotions as they came up. Instead of having a judgmental or harsh reaction to them and trying to repress and push them back down, I welcomed them. The ego wants to minimize discomfort, so it was a big step when I decided I wasn't going to judge myself for how this process looked or felt. My face was wet with tears when I went through the phase of just welcoming it all. I said to myself and the Holy Spirit, "Now, I welcome this even if it doesn't look pretty or feel pretty. No matter how it looks—let's go for the healing!"

The intensity of emotions was so strong. I wondered how people could go for healing while at the same time functioning in the world. How do you keep it together? Are you supposed to, on top of the challenges of keeping a career going and keeping families and interpersonal relationships together, go inward and work on the healing of your mind? It does seem to be that certain things fall apart, melt away, break down, and crumble. But remember, the ego is the one that's interpreting the process every step of the way. It's usually a negative interpretation, "This hurts too much. It's too painful. If God is love, why does it hurt so much in my heart?" The ego gets stirred by these first glimpses of acceptance in your mind because they are pinpricks in its façade.

But once you start the forgiveness process with the Holy Spirit, the more you open up, the more miracles you will start to have. What in the beginning seem like little glimmers of acceptance here and there— which are very important—will start to become more stabilized. First there is an allowance: I allow; I allow; I allow it to look and feel just as it is. I'm not going to judge it. Then after all of that allowance, you come into a true state of acceptance. Another word for that is recognition. It is here that you begin to recognize: "This is really who I am, who I have always been, the One, the One Spirit." The ego is the belief that there is no God. Awakening is the experience that there is only God. You can see that there is zero meeting point between "There is no God" and "There is only God"!

The most difficult phase is the beginning of the turn, but when you really get into the full swing of the turn of the tables and of the mind, everything stabilizes. It feels so natural, so effortless! At that point you don't even need vigilance; it is like being carried along down a peaceful stream. How difficult can that be?

At Heart, We Are Just Forgiving Ourselves

Things that have been difficult to deal with keep coming back at us until we start to realize that the people in our lives were just acting out our beliefs. So, if we seem to be victimized or mistreated or we didn't get the treatment that we felt we deserved, they were simply acting out our unconscious guilt—everything that we have repressed and denied. They were doing a great job of it too; Academy Awards go to your mom and dad for those performances! But the fact is, we weren't remembering them as they truly are; we were just remembering the past grievances that we've kept in our mind and they acted them out.

We are never actually upset by behavior. We are upset by our interpretation of behavior, and we are always responding emotionally to our interpretations. We just perceive what we still have unresolved within our own consciousness or what we still have a grievance on. So, people in our lives are actually doing us a favor. The ones we think are the biggest jerks and the most insensitive people are helping us go past our repression and denial mechanisms. They're acting it out right in front of us so we can allow all of our emotions into awareness. Once they are up in awareness, we can give them over to the Holy Spirit—and have a miraculous experience.

Even just thinking of your mom or dad, or whoever it is that you have a grievance with, activates the memories and the emotions. Working this through is part of the clearing, even if they're not physically in your life. When we dream of them and when we think of them, we can process what they bring up for us. It's part of the healing.

We may not always be aware that whenever we hold a grievance, we are actually holding it against our self. This is because projection makes us see outside what we don't want to see within our own minds and hearts because we're afraid that what we're projecting is actually true about ourselves. This is why, when we forgive, we are really releasing our own soul, our own self.

It takes a lot of energy to hold on to a grievance, energy that could be used for loving instead. If we devote our lives to loving, then the fear and misperceptions of the ego don't have a chance to grow. If we keep our garden weeded, clear, and clean, then we have space for the fruits—and there are plenty of fruits.

Give Beliefs Over to the Holy Spirit

Forgiveness is about really seeing what is in our mind and then releasing it. This is our inner work. You can't actually say to the Holy Spirit, "I have a crazy life. Would You please fix it?" Instead you bring everything that you believe about your life and this world, about time and space back to the Holy Spirit. And when you really do this completely, your issues will disappear. So, in true forgiveness, you go into it with the Holy Spirit, to shine the darkness away, and you are brought back to the experience of this present moment. Bring that darkness to the light. Bring all of your crazy beliefs to the light, and you will see they were just in your imagination. They were just dark dragons, crazy little ideas, you buried and kept hidden. It was just another trick of the ego. It was never real!

Forgiveness is a moment of choosing to be happy instead of being right. Forgiveness is an opportunity to decide for reality anew; it is the moment when you decide for your true Self rather than for an image of yourself.

Forgiveness is to go inward beneath attack thoughts and come into the innocence of who you are, to your divinity. Forgiveness quietly does nothing. It waits and watches, and it doesn't judge. It's just a serene, profound, still state of mind. When forgiveness is our function, we are inherently happy. Forgiveness is our key to happiness!

Imagine you're growing up with your parents, and they say, "What are you going to be when you grow up?" And against all expectations you say, "Happy, happy... I want to be happy!" This isn't temporary happiness associated with specific outcomes. It's not, "I'm happy because I got a raise, found my soulmate, or won the lottery." It's not a temporary kind of happiness. So, the forgiveness practice leads to a very joyful experience because there is no agenda with anything. We can describe the unhappy dream as the misperception, and then the happy, forgiven dream is the touchstone, the closest thing to Heaven on Earth. It's a transformation in mind and in consciousness. It's so close to Heaven that your feet no longer touch the ground, so to speak. You're just carried and lifted!

Forgive and See the World as a Dream

Some people believe that when you start to see the world as a dream or an illusion, you become disinterested or have no sense of love or compassion flowing through you. But it's actually the opposite. The Holy Spirit pours through even more from that state since you don't have an investment in the form being a certain way or looking a certain way. You experience a call for love rather than an attack, and you give what is asked for; you give the love. You do not fall for perception; you do not fall for behavior. As you give love away, you strengthen it, and then you know that you are it, that you are an unlimited extension of divine love.

I was visiting a friend one time when I experienced how the power of forgiveness could transform aggression and rage. This friend and I would watch metaphysical movies and meditate together for hours. She had not mentioned to me that she had gone through a divorce about two years earlier and that her ex-husband was insanely jealous if anyone of the male gender would come near her. One day when we were watching a movie, all of a sudden, a face appeared in the window. It was like a Jack Nicholson movie. His eyes were bulging, and it looked like he was ready to come in with a chainsaw. Then the door blasted open. He was super raging angry, with saliva coming out of his mouth. I had an experience of being in a movie. I didn't even move. I didn't even get up. I just watched this movie as he came over. He was screaming and shouting and grabbed my shirt. I was just observing and noticing. I was experiencing the lesson, "In my defenselessness, my safety lies."

Later, I was walking along a road toward a nearby pine forest to meditate. A car drove up, and it was this man again. He jumped out of the car and came over. He threw my body down on the ground, and my head hit a metal signpost and was bleeding, but I was not feeling any discomfort whatsoever. Then, a car stopped and they said, "What's going on here?"

The man attacking me said, "No! There's no problem." Then he took me back to the house. He started to fumble through the medicine chest, spilling pills all over the place. He was so scared. He was trying to put gauze on my head and give me pills. Then he cracked open and started sharing with me about the pain that he felt about losing his family and all the hurt, and the whole thing turned into a beautiful healing experience. Because I had forgiveness in my heart, used in the deepest way, I could be in true compassion.

Forgiveness can feel profound, very deep, and very mystical. My friend Lisa had a sister who was raped and murdered. After some time, they found and arrested the murderer. He was in jail for many years. Lisa's family and the prosecutor were trying to have him electrocuted for the crime. Even though years earlier, she had come through a deep grieving process around the loss of her beloved sister, Lisa had no grievance against the man. Lisa is joined in the teachings of Jesus Christ on forgiveness and got called to testify in support of the man who murdered her sister. She wasn't condoning any of his actions. Through the years that this man had been in prison, he had been praying and had become very devout. He had been working on his own forgiveness process.

At the courthouse, where her mother, her sister, and the rest of her family were trying to make sure this man was electrocuted, Lisa was there to represent forgiveness. While she was waiting in the hall, she prayed with Jesus. She was looking at the wall, and suddenly Jesus appeared on the wall for her, in the marble. It was a very mystical experience. Then when the time came to testify, she stepped into the elevator, and guess who is in the elevator? The man accused of murdering her sister.

Lisa just gazed at him with love, and the man gazed back. There was a deep sense of recognition and love. Then she gave an amazing testimony. She testified for God, for Christ, and did not hold back one thing. She was not concerned about the outcome of whether they would keep him on death row or whether they would electrocute him. She was there to testify for forgiveness and innocence. She was living the state of forgiveness, she did not mind when she was cross-examined, and she did not mind what happened in the courtroom. She was testifying for forgiveness for all of us. It was very powerful. She went there and with the sharpness of a razor blade, she delivered the clear message of truth and innocence.

Examples of forgiveness show us what becomes possible when we forgive from our hearts. When a friend's daughter was murdered, this friend went into deep prayer. They arrested a man. My friend just kept praying, "What should I do?" and Jesus said "Go to the prison. Go into the cell with this man and say that you love him." This man had murdered his daughter, and he was to go into the prison, into the cell, and just be there with the man. When he went to the prison, he loved this man so thoroughly that this man started writing poetry, doing paintings, and getting into the teachings of A Course in Miracles. Forgiveness is all about seeing beyond the error.

These are strong examples where you can see how your mind might want to twist into rage and blame. Right away, scenarios like these draw images of something evil that you would not want to face. But to me, Lisa, and my other friend, Jesus said, "Take the stranger in." He instructs us to go past all of our thoughts and all of our perceptions that something has been done wrong and to connect in love. Connecting in love is our freedom, connecting in the present. Grievances are always of the past. When we hold a grievance, we remain in prison and so does the whole world. When we forgive, if we go past the grievance and if we see with the eyes of Christ and connect in Christ, we free the whole world.

An experience of true freedom can only come in the present. It can only come with forgiveness. Forgiveness is our sole function—our only gift to the world. We have no life calling other than this. Our life's calling is not to "become" something. In fact, it is the opposite. It is to unwind the false self that we made. And we do that by forgiving it, by forgiving our belief in it. We are no longer bound by fear, guilt, and doubt when we have fully looked at all of our beliefs, down to the core belief in separation, and released them. This is the ultimate unlearning and unwinding of the mind that will lead to a life of blissful freedom and joy.

Forgiveness sweeps away distortion and opens the hidden altar to the truth. For here, and only here, is peace of mind restored, for this is the dwelling place of God Himself. With complete forgiveness, you will see that no one can be hurt, and once you get in touch with the deep presence, all things are equally acceptable. In the perception of forgiveness, of the gentle grace of love that you are, everything is seen as whole. And it is so relaxing in that holistic view that you can literally be carried through the day, letting the wind take you like a feather. Like in the opening scene of *Forrest Gump*, the feather is not trying to direct the wind, and likewise Forrest cluelessly goes with the flow.

EXERCISE: Release and Experience True Forgiveness

To listen to a recorded version of this exercise, go to http://www.newharbinger.com/41870.

Ask the Holy Spirit to guide you now as you get quiet. Allow your mind to become very silent and still. Take a moment to think about a person in your life who has been a target of your judgments and your grievances, someone whom you haven't yet forgiven, someone who upsets you or irritates you. This could be someone near or far, someone related to you, a person that you engage with frequently, or a person who has passed away. It could be someone you have had a difficult and unloving experience with. It is very likely that this person has already come to your mind. This person will be the one you ask Spirit to help you to see through loving eyes.

Part 1. Journaling for Forgiveness

1. Describe a situation involving this person in which a grievance or unforgiving thought obscures the miracle from you.

2. Observe your mind to see what conclusions you have drawn about this person that are all based on the past. How are you judging this person? List everything in your journal.

3. Observe your mind to see what conclusions you have drawn about yourself in relation to this person. Are you still judging yourself this way? List the ways.

4. Imagine meeting this person again and spend a few minutes with them in your mind. Use your journal to explore any additional thoughts, judgments, or emotions about them and yourself, being very honest to allow subtle and hidden thoughts to arise into awareness. Take your time in your reflections. Get them all down on paper, and when you feel complete, offer all your thoughts to the Spirit and move on to part 2.

Part 2. Reflecting on Forgiveness

Reflect on this for a while: "The miracle enables you to see your friend without his or her past. Let no dark cloud out of your past obscure him or her from you, for truth lies only in the present, and you will find it there if you seek it there." This person is not your enemy; rather, they will help you experience the miracle of forgiveness. In truth, this is always someone you wish to love peacefully, yet are hindered from doing so by holding onto your existing judgments, grievances, upsets, and regrets.

"Now" has no meaning to the ego. This is why you heal as you release the investment in past and future. Today, give no heed to the shadowy figures from the past. Now is the time when you are absolved of all past. Turn to the Holy Spirit to let Him guide you in this practice. Today forgiveness is your function. Forgive the past and the belief in the future. Today, have a change of interpretation about time and its function. Open up to the present moment!

Part 3. Meditating to Welcome Forgiveness

Practicing forgiveness has the potential to completely transform your relationships. For this meditation, begin by allowing your mind to become very silent and still. Think about the importance of what you are about to do and the healing and peace that you are welcoming.

Witness your hurts and grievances as you bring them to mind once more. Hold this person again in your mind, as you now currently see them. Review the difficulties you have had, the pain and suffering you thought they caused you, any neglect, and all the little and larger hurts you believe they inflicted. You will regard this person's body with its flaws and better points as well, and you will think of their mistakes or even of their "sins."

Now, begin to open to the possibility that your faulty perception can be transformed. Practice seeing this person in a new light, try to find some light in them, and allow this light to grow in the picture that you see before you. Ask the Holy Spirit to help you see beyond the fixed image you hold. As you allow yourself to open your mind and be guided to see this person differently, you will begin to see the light from behind the illusion. In doing so, you free this person and yourself of the dark images you have placed upon them. Take some time to truly allow the light in. In gratitude, allow yourself to accept this new perception and to see this person in their true identity, in the light and without any reference from the past. As you do this, you also see the truth in yourself, which is light, and it becomes evident to you that changing your perception about the other person sets you free along with them. This person has given you the opportunity to see the power and the release that comes from transforming your judgments to a loving, accepting witness of the truth that is in you and everyone else. Take some time to rest in the quiet resolution that you've found. Take all the time you need and bask in the light of the miracle.

And now, meditate on this poem. Read it slowly, you may read it aloud, copy it in your journal, or post it on your refrigerator. Do anything that brings its message deeply into your mind.

Use no relationship to hold you to the past,

but with each one, each day, be born again.

A minute, even less, will be enough to free you from the past,

and give your mind in peace to the present moment.

When everyone is welcome to you as you would have yourself

be welcome to God and your Self, you will feel no guilt.

For you will have forgiven.

Forgiveness Is the Love that Calls Forth Happiness

Wouldn't it be wonderful to experience gliding through your life like it's a peaceful dream, where you are just delighted and fully accepting of yourself and others? In this world of dreams, your goal can become the transformational forgiveness of your perception from a nightmare to a happy dream. The happy dream in simple terms is a dream of nonjudgment. Human beings organize the world they see and their lives on Earth based on many beliefs. Forgiveness, which is what the happy dream is about, is like a giant, all-encompassing belief. In fact, it's such a large belief that, like Jonah and the whale, it literally swallows up all the other ones. This means that with forgiveness, you have the experience that all specific beliefs are completely untrue. So, forgiveness puts you in a state of complete open-mindedness, acceptance, and all-inclusiveness.

Practically, this means that you won't ever get into an argument again because you know that there are no specific beliefs that are truer than others; they are all equally false. All the labels and all the things that people seem to defend, such as different cultures, religions, and beliefs associated with different ethnicities, will have zero significant differences to you. You will have an experience of the unified awareness in which everything is one. Everything is mind, and you're identified as that. You've completely transcended arguments, debates, the belief in right and wrong, and opinions.

When you come from a place of forgiveness, you come to see that all meaning is in your heart, and you will bring that beautiful meaning to everything that you look upon. You take that love in your heart, and you let it pour out on absolutely everything. Beauty is in the eye of the beholder, and when you're beholding with the eyes of love, you can't help but to see and extend that love.

Many witnesses are called forth. This is the way the dream lights up. Witnesses of love, peace, and harmony begin to flood the mind. Witnesses of love replace witnesses of fear, guilt, shame, and pain. Witnesses of happiness, joy, and freedom sprinkle throughout the mind and the dreamscape.

My friend had an experience of this as he was walking down the street right after the Twin Towers fell on 9/11 in New York. He was walking along and was very happy, doing his *Course in Miracles* lesson of the day. All of a sudden, he had a doubt thought, *What if my joy disturbs these people's sorrow?* This doubt thought brought about witnesses of fear, and all of a sudden, he could smell the stank and see all the misery. He perceived the mourning of a particular man who was walking across the street. He caught himself and thought, *I'd better continue on with my lesson of the day.* Then, remembering his Course lesson for the day, his perception shifted, and the man who looked sorrowful, now looked bright, clear, and happy. He went over, looked my friend right in the eyes, and started rapping the following powerful words: "I can see...by the way that you feel...that you know...that none of this is real!" He became a witness of joy and lightness.

Through forgiveness, you just emanate and radiate the truth. This is where the miracle appears in awareness. You stay in the truth of innocence and refuse to see your brother or sister as something they are not. And when you hold this presence and vision of innocence, they are lifted up to remember who they are too. It's the most loving and compassionate experience ever. And it's truly shared!

CHAPTER 17

EXTENDING FROM WITHIN

True giving and true service is with the Holy Spirit; it is an experience not in form. It is a state of mind where you experience what you truly give. It is so different from the world's concept of giving, where the gift is something in form that you would lose as a consequence of giving it. If you give it away, it's gone, it's used up, kiss it good-bye, and you'll never see it again. And if you keep giving that way, they'll have more, and you'll have less. You can see how the ego finds giving very strange.

True Giving

There is a powerful teaching in *A Course in Miracles*: "To have, give all to all." This teaching contradicts the entire ego belief system. So, what is true giving, true extending? The Holy Spirit says just give me your mind, and I will take care of everything else. If you're worried, sad, or tired, you are not really giving. But if you are inspired and connected to your Divine Source, you give true and amazing inspiration; you share joy, peace, and love. There is no tiredness or loss, only extension. This is because it is by sharing God's gifts of joy and love that you keep them. This can only be understood through experience. "All that I give is given to myself." This teaching of the Holy Spirit is a very strange notion to the ego. But to us, it's the perfect answer. "All that I give is given to myself" is a divine principle. It's the experience of having a relationship with God.

Withholding something in the present is not the way of the Spirit. Planning for the future is not the way of the Spirit. We've all been into withholding in one way or another. "Don't put all your eggs in one basket." "Always save for a rainy day." We have been taught to withhold, that it is prudent to withhold, even in relationships. "Don't give it all away, string them along a little bit, make them work for it, make them chase, and make them pursue." Who taught us this stuff? If God gives His love unconditionally, then why wouldn't we want to give it too?

We associate giving with loss and sacrifice. But from a miracle-minded perspective, giving is completely different; giving in form is irrelevant. It comes down to not actually knowing your best interest and opening up to being guided in terms of form. When you give miracles away, the giver and the receiver both have more! We know that about love: when you extend love to somebody, you feel more love in your heart. This is the way that we were created by God: to give love just like He does. As soon as the ego tries to put a price on this, it is not love anymore. It is just another exchange.

Developing trust is to learn to give as God gives: give love and grow in trust. As you extend love, you will experience that the universe is giving you everything back, and you will naturally grow in trust. In the end, from trusting and allowing the support that's given by the Holy Spirit from moment to moment, you will come to experience that giving and receiving are the same. True receiving is true giving. That realization is nothing less than the awakening itself. When you are receiving Spirit from moment to moment, you are also giving Spirit. That is the nature of Spirit. It is not personal, and it is always extending. The experience of trust, joy, contentment, and peace is a sign that you are in touch with Spirit, and being in touch with Spirit is true giving. Receiving and giving become one.

When your dreams become happy, you know that you're just at the point of getting your final lesson. This final insight is learning that what you have is what you are. This means that "having" is an experience of your divine Self—safe, free, and at home. Remember that in oneness, there is no difference between having and being as there is in the dream. In the state of being, the mind gives everything always. To have is no longer associated with an ownership of things or of having self-importance. Without attachments, you become free. That's why Buddha taught to empty your mind of everything you think that you think and everything you think you are. He was saying let go of the false identifications that relate to this world and come into a still, tranquil mind, which is beyond this world. That's what Jesus was teaching as well. Whereas Buddha might have called it the void, Jesus would have said, "Yes, go into the void and come through the void to the Kingdom of Heaven, to full joy, to full happiness, to the fullness of Holy Spirit." That's what this journey is all about!

How to Be Truly Helpful

We all want to do good. And we all do what we believe makes us happy. Kahlil Gibran wrote a beautiful little book called *The Prophet*. He said that when you work, you should work with joy and love. True service can be an opportunity to let the personality be washed away. There are many volunteers of service all over the world. Millions of people are involved in service, but many of them experience burnout. They burn out in their volunteerism. How does this happen? The ego must be involved. The ego will try to hijack service for its own purposes: "Save the hungry, save the poor, save Mother Earth, save the dolphins, save the whales for God's sake, save the tuna! Save the environment. Save your country." They get very angry about the obstacles in the way and eventually angry at themselves for not being able to cure the problems. This is not going to work. The ego has hijacked the concept of service. If service does not lead to joy, you are following the imposter, the ego.

When I was growing up, people told me to always look out for number one. And I said, "Who is number one?" They said, "It is you. It is yourself, David." They meant the personality self. But when you go into true service, you are turning that advice around. Always look out for the One—the One Source. As you give yourself over to this devotion, the Holy Spirit will give you every step so as to serve in the best way to heal and undo the blocks to love's awareness in your mind.

Everything that we do in forgiveness is so that we can remove those blocks to love, so we can love God and our neighbor as our self. Literally, as our self, not like we are loving somebody else—we just radiate this Self-love. The more we are able to forgive illusions, the more love can pour through our consciousness and the more aware we become of how powerful that love is. We cannot be conduits for Christ, conduits for Spirit, when we are fearful. This means a moment-to-moment practice of suspending our judgments, doubt, and fear. The light will wait until we are clear and calm.

A Course in Miracles offers this prayer: "I am here only to be truly helpful. I am here to represent Him Who sent me. I do not have to worry about what to say or what to do, because He Who sent me will direct me. I am content to be wherever He wishes, knowing He goes there with me. I will be healed as I let Him teach me to heal." That is such a beautiful prayer. I used that prayer every time I would go through a doorway, entering a situation. Whether I was going to the grocery store, to the laundromat, to A Course in Miracles group, to visit my grandmother, to pick up cat food, or wherever, I would just pause and silently let the Spirit give me that prayer because it would orient my mind to what I was really going through the door for. I oriented my mind to being there to be truly helpful rather than to just accomplishing tasks.

I wasn't there to get in and out of the grocery store as fast as I could with the best prices and with the best ingredients. That was the old pattern. I missed a lot of holy encounters and wasted a lot of time when I was rushing through, jumping from line to line, trying to save time, reading ingredients on packages, and comparing prices. Grocery shopping was a long, tedious thing before the Holy Spirit got a hold of me. Then I would pray the prayer. I would go in, usually get some items, but I would be smiling, meeting people in the aisles, and talking to people. If the Holy Spirit guided me to a long line, I would go in the long line and have a wonderful discussion. Even if the cashier was new and she rang up the wrong price or she dropped the change, I had all the time in the world, and I could tell her everything is okay.

You become patient and loving when you say this prayer. You become helpful and you're there to extend the attitude. You're not really there to buy the groceries; that's secondary. Then you start to apply this true helpfulness to everything, even at work and with your relationships. You start saying, "Oh, this is the healing in my mind; this is what my body is supposed to be used for." You get your mind turned around the right way, and then life gets really gentle, graceful, and flowing.

When I was in Bali, I was paying for some groceries, and the cashier gave me a piece of candy shaped like a heart. It had the words "I love you" on it, and the cashier did the *namaste* (a greeting of love and respect that includes a slight bow with the hands pressed together) to me. I thought, *This is the way to go grocery shopping, instead of "Have a nice day," and boom, on to the next one.* It was presence; it was so beautiful. That gives us an idea how we can live our lives with presence, with grace, with love, and with kindness coming from our heart.

Everything Comes from Devotion; You Don't Need to Figure it Out!

In the process of waking up, everyone is given a part to play. But it's given from the inside. You don't even have to figure it out. You can trust and relax. You can start right now; you can just take some deep breaths and say, "I don't have to figure my life out." And another deep breath, "I don't have to fix my life." Another deep breath, "I don't have to fix my body." Another deep breath, "I don't even have to figure out how to maintain this body because when I let go of the ego, everything is given, everything that the body could need or use is given freely." Breathe. A very difficult question that we ponder on Earth is *What am I going to do for a living?* Your living can be given to you moment by moment. All you need to do is turn your life over to the presence of the Holy Spirit, and if there's a word to say or if there's a smile to give, it will happen. Whatever you need will be given!

Let your life to be a life of devotion, with integrity, so you can—in a friendly way—say, "Come along, come and see, come in closer." It's about transparency. The way you live your life can be extremely transparent because when your mind holds only what you think with God, you have nothing to hide or protect. You can afford to be a really open book when you live a devoted life. You can say to people, come, come closer, come as close as you want.

Just Extend the Joy Regardless of Differences

I love traveling around the world meeting so many different people. At times somebody will come up to me and say, "I'm an atheist." And we just have the most wonderful time together. We don't even have to go into the issue of belief or unbelief. We just share the joy and the love. And the Spirit uses whatever words are needed—if I'm talking to a scientist, I just zoom right into quantum physics, and they love it. They light up. And if I'm with somebody who identifies as a Christian, it's so biblical. And they're like, "Yeah! Praise God!" When I'm with Buddhists, it comes out in the Buddhist way. They say, "Yeah!" We're meant to connect and join and rejoice with everybody, not to split hairs over illusory beliefs. In the end, who cares if they believe in God or they don't? I just rejoice in love no matter what they believe. In this sense, service is the same as nonjudgment and true complete open-mindedness. So, we can be truly helpful and connect with everyone and feel connected without any barriers.

One time, I went to an American Indian reservation, and I met a teenager along with his mother and father. The father was totally into the Native American tradition. The mother had been raised Catholic. She was totally into Jesus and had no interest at all in the Native American tradition. I could feel a big disconnect between the parents and the teenager. I went on a walk with the father, and the Holy Spirit poured through me completely using Native American symbols. It was all about no boundaries, everything is connected, and everything is the Spirit. Then, I went with the mother, I spoke using Christian terms, and she was just so happy. Her love of Jesus was so strong; I had such a connection with her. Then I went with the teenage son, and he was not interested in Native American culture or Jesus at all. He was into *The*

Matrix. And we shared a deep connection because it was all spoken in Matrix terms: Neo, Morpheus, Trinity, the sentinels, and so forth. Everybody has their own perceptions, they relate to Source in their own way, and they have deep experiences, but the semantics are completely different. The Holy Spirit is not bothered by the semantics or the seeming beliefs. And that's why we train our minds: so we can be fully present, completely, with whomever we are with. Because it's really our self, and all we really desire is love and connection. And the Spirit knows the way. The Spirit will inspire us and show us. It could be through music; it could be through anything.

When you realize that the body is a communication device, you see that you're meant to smile through it, laugh through it, hug through it, and speak kind and gentle words through it. You're meant to let the wisdom of the whole universe pour through the body. This way you're going to teach exactly what you would learn. Just like when you learn to ride a bike; you need practice. Nobody just hops on the bike and goes riding the first time. There is a need for practice, sometimes with training wheels. You have to be gentle with yourself when you start to teach what you would learn. If you have love inside and you bottled it up for some reason, maybe you've been afraid and asking, "What will it mean if I am loving? What will the world say? What will people expect of me if I'm loving? Maybe they will get the wrong idea about me." But if you had it bottled up, you've got to let it out because that extension of love is your purpose. Your happiness depends on extending love. You want to be inspired by what is inside of you. You want it to come out and extend through you.

Then your perception starts to expand, and you start to have experiences that you are more than the body. You realize that the body is not who you are, that it is just an instrument that is being used in your awakening. And then as you go even deeper, you'll start to have communion experiences and mystical experiences that actually start to transcend the body entirely. You may start to have lucid dream experiences where during your nighttime dreams, you are so lucid and aware that you're dreaming that even when there is a monster, a dragon, or a tsunami, you're just smiling and laughing because you know it's a dream. You're grateful as you know that you're dreaming, and you're not at the mercy of whatever seems to be going on. And then it will start to transfer to your daily life as well, where you have this sense of being, the sense that you're watching or observing life.

MEDITATION: Diving Under This World to the Light

To listen to a recorded version of this meditation, go to http://www .newharbinger.com/41870.

To be able to extend Spirit from within, you need to turn all your attention inward to an experience of being connected to Source. Make sure you have a space where you will not be disturbed for a while. Take a moment to get in touch with your thoughts. Get in touch with your emotions, invite them into full awareness. Let this meditation take you deep into your heart and your being.

Take a moment now to just watch what is in your consciousness. Watch the passing panorama. Observe the thoughts. This is your arena for healing. You are looking into the mind. You are observing consciousness. Open up to a purification of consciousness.

Look at the contents of your consciousness very directly. You are looking at your life, your mind. It is not about an environment; it is not about people, places, events, or situations. It is about beginning to be very, very aware of the contents of consciousness. Imagine your consciousness as a radio station; you must pay attention, you must be aware of what is coming through in the broadcast.

Just for a little while, turn away from being so plugged in to the thinking of the world. Turn away from just reacting and responding to people, places, and events. This moment, right now, is all there is. For just a moment, allow yourself to see that all remembrances of the past, and all projections and anticipations of the future, are but a game of folly, a ruse, to keep you distracted from this very moment.

I invite you to sink deep, deep within your mind, to sink beneath these layers of thoughts, relaxing very deeply. I invite you to open to the stillness and the presence that is your very identity. For a moment now, you need not put your attention on the things of this world, the sights and sounds. Give yourself permission to let all this go.

You don't have to be a participant in the world of events, you can just observe; watch. No longer are you in the rat race, in the busyness, the hurriedness, or the hustle and bustle of time and space, people, and places.

Now, very gently, stop, drop, and watch. Feel the deep peace that's there when there is no forcing, no pushing, and no striving. Just sink down into a state of mind in which there is no effort, only pure acceptance. Acceptance and rest. Accept everything as it is, right now.

Just watch your thoughts as if they are a parade going by. You are not in the parade, you just watch.

Sink into deep, deep peace. You are with the Holy Spirit. Sink beneath the belief in parts and particulars and situations and specifics. Deep, deep, deep into the mind, until you feel very light. And feel the light that's there. There is a light beyond thoughts, emotions and beliefs.

Be a passerby. That is your contribution and your sacred purpose. The truth of your spiritual identity is abiding in grace in the Kingdom of Heaven or oneness forever. I am calling you out of the world of perception; I am calling you to rest deep within, beloved child of God.

Today embrace one purpose. Today, experience it. Rest in peace. Rest in the present moment. Rejoice in happiness and in being as God created you.

Amen.

Let this experience direct you to your inner space of healing and quiet and take a little time purely for yourself. Realize that no time could ever be spent better. In quiet rest, allow yourself the gift of release.

Love Extends by Its Nature

We want to have an attitude of being so focused on the presence of love that everything and everyone is touched by that love. We call on and welcome the Holy Spirit to flood our life, and love and blessing will flow through us. This is what we want our whole life to be. We want everything to be lit up around us, reflecting all the love and blessings of the Holy Spirit!

All of us are being called as miracle workers, and we cannot turn away in embarrassment thinking that we must have been chosen wrongly. We will be content with nothing less than being miracle workers. We are all saints in training, and even though the training can seem pretty rough at times, we will succeed because God's plan for salvation must succeed. God's plan for salvation does not require egos. But the presence of love is so strong inside of us that we are assured of success. So, we support each other in releasing any dark emotions, in laughing together, singing together, and praying together. This is the calling of our heart, and we are joined hand in hand!

Eventually, as you step back from the ego and share an allowance for the Holy Spirit, you hold a space of love and nonjudgment in your communication: no criticism, no crosstalk, no advice-giving. There's a feeling of love and acceptance, which is fundamental in clearing out your consciousness of all judgments and grievances. This allowance and acceptance of everything to be as it is leads to constant happiness. When you're always happy, there's also openness to say, "Okay Spirit, what would you have me do?" And it's a feeling of "Give it away to everyone in the whole universe. Help make spirituality fun for everyone." What does that look like? We dance, and we sing. We watch amazing movies that open up our hearts. We have beautiful experiential gatherings. It involves deep heart-to-heart talks. It involves seeing friends in every direction that you look; even the snowflakes become your friends. You feel connected to the plants, animals, and people. And you laugh a lot. Every day there's laughter. Not one single day goes by without laughter. And it all comes from inside of your heart.

During this last phase, there is a lot of extending the gift because once you experience the gift of love, it automatically gives itself away. So, there are many collaborative encounters that are part of giving this gift. And your words can be of quantum physics, of poetry, or of song lyrics. It comes in so many different ways that you never know what it will be. This is a way of living; it's a state of mind! And the form is not important anymore. Even the words are not important. You just sparkle and shine.

It's time to give gratitude to what's real, what's true, and all the reflections of this love that are all around. You'll find that, as you open your heart and open your mind, the love of God is reflected in everything and everyone that you perceive. In every direction that you look, it is sanctified in your heart; it is a deep, unspeakable love. If you are not experiencing this love, this boundless vast love, then stay open, stay open to the laughter, to the peace, and to the signs and symbols that are calling you each moment and this day forever to awake and be glad. Love is always either in your heart or on its way!

LIVING IN FREEDOM

When it comes to healing, you aren't limited by anything. You can use whatever opens your heart—poetry, music, dance, or deep heart-to-heart conversations. You don't need to let things like conditioning and opinions stop you from coming into an experience once you open your mind to overlook and undo your patterns and fears. You are here to have an experience of your connectedness. There are pathways to God that don't use words, where you sink deeply inward beneath the thoughts and the words and come into a direct experience of Source. We can all drop into this experience, where we're totally connected; there's no separation at all.

Peace is an experience of communion with Spirit, our true Self. Communion goes beyond and must transcend the body. Communion is the light of love. It is perfect oneness and eternal tranquil peace. It is the return to what is real. And this is the unity and purity of heart that Christ, your true, awake Self, radiates forever. There is an endless freedom that comes from pulling back your projections from the world and owning your mind's power as the cause of all that you perceive and experience. As such, peace comes from transcending the body, the world, and the whole cosmos—the dream that was made in projection. This is freedom.

This freedom is the only thing in the world that can bring joy. It is given by the Holy Spirit. It encompasses the entire cosmos—all the galaxies, black holes, stars, and planets; it's healed perception and the result of a forgiven mind. This is a happy, perfect answer to a very crazy problem. There may appear to be many steps to reach this freedom, but when you do, you realize that there were no steps at all. When you arrive at the end of dreams, at the end of all illusions, God wakes you gently from this last and happiest of dreams, to your true Self. Thoughts of the ego can't even enter your pristine, holy mind here. The light becomes so strong and so bright that thoughts of temptation to be otherwise can't even enter!

The healing of the mind is an ongoing adventure. It is a journey of releasing false images, identity associations, and self-concepts. Situations and encounters in your life will act out anything that you have pushed out of awareness, but you are opening up to and approaching a state of all-inclusion, a state of nonattachment and nonaffiliation, a state of stillness.

The Holy Spirit flows through you with loving acceptance for the whole universe in this state. This communion with Spirit can still involve words, but mostly you will know it as a presence of love that casts out all fear. It is an experience that leads you to say that you've never met a stranger. All the things that seem to be sticking points become irrelevant—including those around religion. The experience of religion becomes an experience of peace of mind. Hindu, Muslim, or Christian— it doesn't matter because peace is an experience that literally transcends all the theologies and all the concepts.

In this freedom is a feeling of Home. It's a presence of being Home. It's a state where Heaven and Earth cease to exist as separate states. Heaven is here, and it is now. That's what makes it a happy state; it's not a future state. It's not something that you hope and wish for. It's an actual state. Traveling around the world and meeting people from different cultures with different languages and traditions has been a treat for me. It's a divine fiesta. It's an ongoing party because there is no point to be made or proven.

That's the fun of it! There is absolutely no point. When people say to me, "What's the point of this world?" I say, "Really, there is no point." God's will for us is perfect happiness, so if you really had to come up with something like a point or a purpose, it would have to be happiness. We align our mind to the purpose of the Holy Spirit and that brings peace and happiness. The light of the Holy Spirit simply is. When the resistance to peace has been removed, the light shines unobstructed in awareness.

When we take this journey with the Holy Spirit, we are not lacking at all and therefore don't want for anything. The first line of the twenty-third Psalm is "The Lord is my shepherd, I shall not want." This line seems to contain everything because it explains the feeling of fulfilment where in every moment, everything is given. Everything is in divine order. Everything is perfect. Nothing is lacking. So, there is no sense of ambition, of trying to strive for something, and you don't have any future goals. Contentment is the pervasive feeling of fulfilment where the world need be no different than it is. No situation that you perceive need be different than it is.

The whole journey of healing and awakening is contained in the forgiveness process. Enlightenment, or to know thyself, is the completion of this process. Enlightenment is at the top of the mountain; it is at the pinnacle of this whole effort. At this point, the Holy Spirit ceases to be a messenger or a bridge. The Holy Spirit is no longer an agent or a necessary communication link, as we are one. We are Spirit, one with God.

After reading this book and doing the exercises, you may have now found that you can trust that there is one real purpose for everything, which results in pure joy and peace of mind. This is the mystical experience of healing and awakening. There are no consequences to letting go of illusions, only a glorious experience of what is real and what is natural in this very moment. Go through the void and come into the allness of being! The means is the miracle!

Now, you are free to arise in joy for dramas and games have ended! Never need they be summoned again into awareness. Be glad for their passing and remember the gift that forgiveness offered. The blanket of peace softly spreads across the Earth, and you rest in a tranquil mind that remains invulnerable forever.

For a miracle is now.

It stands already here,

in present grace,

within the only interval of time

that sin and fear have overlooked,

but which is all there is to time.

GRATITUDE AND ACKNOWLEDGMENTS

This book, like every aspect of the nonprofit Foundation for the Awakening Mind, is the fruit of love. I offer my deep appreciation to the Holy Spirit and New Harbinger Publications and everyone whose passion made this material available in book form so that many can benefit from this inner wisdom. I wish to acknowledge the countless hours of effort contributed by the Foundation for the Awakening Mind publishing team. Your inspired contributions made this book possible. Thanks to Jenny and Greg Donner for putting the team together and for your steadfast leadership and continuous collaborations. I am forever grateful.

RESOURCES

Levels of Mind: http://levelsofmind.com. Details the levels of mind process using both text and video.

Spiri, Your Spiritual Assistant: http://www.facebook.com/Your.Spiri/. This "bot" has been developed out of the Instrument for Peace and Levels of Mind and is an interactive guide to release upsets (which were explored throughout the book). It is the modern version of the instrument for peace! For more on Spiri, visit http://spiri.ai/.

Living Miracles: http://livingmiracles.org. This free website allows an interested individual to sign up for a monthly newsletter, explore volunteering opportunities, and link in more closely with Living Miracles. It includes a free online listing of events (both local and online) taking place within the Living Miracles community.

A Course in Miracles Online: http://acourseinmiraclesnow.com. This free, valuable resource contains *A Course in Miracles* in its entirety, in both a text version and an audio version (read by me). There is a useful search tool for those looking to identify specific content and ideas presented in the Course.

30 Day UYM Experience: http://circle.livingmiraclescenter.org/uym 30day. We call this program the Unwind Your Mind Experience. Subscribers receive thirty days of emails, resources, songs, prayers, and meditations, and have access to a private online support group, along with online movies every Saturday. All of this is offered for free and is Course-based.

Home in Christ: http://the-christ.net. This free website warmly welcomes individuals with Christian upbringing into the ACIM community by offering Sunday Services and a range of resources that are less metaphysical and more devotional.

Non-Dual Teacher David Hoffmeister: http://nondualteacher.com. This free website has a collection of my talks on video that omit the concepts of religion in ACIM yet emphasize the metaphysical and modern nonduality concepts of ACIM.

David Hoffmeister's YouTube Channel: http://www.youtube.com/user/DavidHoffmeister. This free YouTube channel has hundreds of hours of video footage of my recorded talks and teachings, and a large number of videos have been subtitled in foreign languages as well.

NOTES

4   It is only in this moment that we are truly able to perform the miracle of forgiveness.   Forgiveness of illusion is our one-way track out of fear and into freedom. See chapter 16.

5   The Holy Spirit's thought system, on the other hand, is something we are relearning to think and operate from, bridging the gap of separation in our disconnected hearts and minds and allowing us to remember our true identity as Divine Spirit. For a thorough description of mind versus   Spirit the way it is used in this book, see "Mind—Spirit" C-1 in *A Course in Miracles* (ACIM), Third Edition Combined Volume. Mill Valley, CA: Foundation for Inner Peace, 2007.

12   *In no situation that arises do you realize the outcome that would make you happy.*   ACIM, W-pI.24.1:1.

12   *Everything is for your own best interests.*   ACIM, W-pI.25.1:5.

12   All things work together for good with no exceptions except in the ego's judgment.   ACIM, T-4.V.1:1–2.

13   *Into eternity, where all is one, there crept a tiny, mad idea, at which the Son of God remembered not to laugh. In his forgetting did the thought become a serious idea, and possible of both accomplishment and real effects. Together, we can laugh them both away, and understand that time cannot intrude upon eternity. It is a joke to think that time can come to circumvent eternity, which means there is no time.*   ACIM, T-27.VIII.6.

13   *It is reasonable to ask how the mind could ever have made the ego. In fact, it is the best question you could ask. There is, however, no point in giving an answer in terms of the past because the past does not matter, and history would not exist if the same errors were not being repeated in the present.*   ACIM, T-4.II.1:1–3.

15   We can't solve our problems with the same level of thinking that created them.   This popular saying has been widely attributed to Einstein, but its exact origin is unknown.

17   Exercise: Moving from Opinions to Prayer. *Prayer* simply means intention or desire. Here it refers to the desire for truth, Spirit.

18   It states that if you find resistance strong and dedication weak, you should not fight yourself.   *ACIM*, T-30.I.1:6–7.

22   Lesson 2 of *A Course in Miracles* teaches that you have given everything you see all the meaning that it has for you.   *ACIM*, W-pI.2.

23   *My thoughts are images that I have made.*   *ACIM*, W-pI.15.

24   *A Course in Miracles* teaches us that without attack thoughts in our mind, we cannot see a world of attack.   *ACIM*, W-pI.55.3.(23):3.

26   With the help of the miracle, the mind is turned right side up, away from its former upside-down way of being, experiencing, and operating.   The Levels of Mind Diagram, Foundation for the Awakening Mind, https:// livingmiraclescenter.org/doc/levelsofmind.pdf.

28   *That's not the reason why. The problem's not out there; you have to look inside.*   Resta Burnham. 2000–2002. "That's Not the Reason Why." *Music of Christ*. Cincinnati, OH: Foundation for the Awakening Mind. http://livingmiracles.org/thats-not-the-reason-why.

30   Watch the Disney movie, *The Kid*.   Jon Turteltaub, director. 2000. *The Kid*, Walt Disney Pictures.

32   *It is from your peace of mind that a peaceful perception of the world arises.*   *ACIM*, W-pI.34.1:4.

32   *The miracle is a lesson in total perception.*   *ACIM*, T-7.IX.7:4.

41   This means that the experience of guilt is solely a result of the purpose the ego gives to things.   The ego's purpose for the body is pride, pleasure, and attack.   *ACIM*, T-6.V.A.5.

46   *For you must learn that guilt is always totally insane, and has no reason.*   *ACIM*, T-13.X.6:3.

46   *All anger is nothing more than an attempt to make someone feel guilty.*   *ACIM*, T-15.VII.10:3.

46   *A Course in Miracles* states that guilt feelings are just a sign that we don't know that God Himself orders our thoughts and also that we believe we can think apart from Him.   *ACIM*, T-5.V.7:1–6.

48   Jesus told the parable of the prodigal son, where the one son left after asking for his inheritance.   *The Holy Bible, New King James Version*. 1979. Luke 15:11–32. Nashville, TN: Thomas Nelson Publishing.

49   Whenever the pain of guilt or the desire to be right arises, remember that if you yield to it, you are deciding against your happiness, and you will not learn how to be happy.   *ACIM*, T-14.III.3.

51 I am the work of God, and His work is wholly lovable and wholly loving. This is how a man must think of himself in his heart because this is what he is.   *ACIM*, T-1.III.2:3.

54 But the need to be defensive can only come when we have identified with an illusion of our self.   *ACIM*, T-22.V.6:1.

55 When the Self is realized and there is an experience of pure oneness, there are no longer any experiences of private thoughts, yet the condition of being in this world is to believe in those thoughts. In fact, they are believed to be the only reality.   *ACIM*, W-pI52.5(10):2–3.

56 If we had to give a definition of God's will for us, it would be perfect happiness.   *ACIM*, W-pI.101.

57 *And yet it is only the hidden that can terrify, not for what it is, but for its hiddenness.*   *ACIM*, T-14.VI.1:4.

61 Every thought you keep hidden shuts communication off.   *ACIM*, T-15. IV.7–8.

62 This holy instant, this moment, is the recognition that all minds are in communication.   *ACIM*, T-15.IV.6.

67 This is because thoughts and images of forms are one and the same.   *ACIM*, W-pI.15.

68 You will let Spirit decide for you.   *ACIM*, T-5.VII.6:11.

69 *Today I will make no decisions by myself.*   *ACIM*, T-30.I.2:2.

74 The question becomes, Can I shift my perception and come to the trust that leads to an experience of literally being sustained by the love of God?   *ACIM*, W-pI.50.

79 There came a point when Jesus said to me, "Okay, that's the last job you will have working for a paycheck and reciprocity."   "Reciprocity" is the practice of exchanging things with others for mutual benefit. It occurs when the contribution of each party meets the expectation of the other party. It stems from an idea of lack; that there is only so much money, time and other means to go around. A belief in risking loss is behind reciprocity. But God's unlimited love is free and is what truly sustains us.

80 *the son of man has no place to lay his head.*   *The Holy Bible*, NKJV, Luke 9:58.

81 *"Except ye become as little children..."*   *ACIM*, T-1.V.3:4.

88 The practice is to come back to the mind, to come to a deeper point of not knowing how or what to judge, to the place inside where we actually don't know what is good or bad.   See the "Moving from Opinions to Prayer" exercise in chapter 1.

88　*...In no situation that arises do you realize the outcome that would make you happy.*　ACIM, W-pI.24:1.

89　*I do not perceive my own best interests. In no situation that arises do you realize the outcome that would make you happy. Therefore, you have no guide to appropriate action, and no way of judging the result. What you do is determined by your perception of the situation, and that perception is wrong.*　ACIM, W-pI.24.1:1–3.

90　*You will also recognize that many of your goals are contradictory, that you have no unified outcome in mind, and that you must experience disappointment in connection with some of your goals however the situation turns out.*　ACIM, W-pI.24.6:2.

91　*What could you not accept, if you but knew that everything that happens, all events, past, present and to come, are gently planned by One Whose only purpose is your good? Perhaps you have misunderstood His plan, for He would never offer pain to you. But your defenses did not let you see His loving blessing shine in every step you ever took. While you made plans for death, He led you gently to eternal life.*　ACIM, W-pI.135.18.

91　It's like the movie *August Rush*, which is a beautiful example of how everything is orchestrated perfectly even when things don't look good. August stays committed to his calling and inner certainty.　David Hoffmeister. 2017. *Movie Watcher's Guide to Enlightenment.* Kamas, UT: Living Miracles Publications. See also https://mwge.org.

97　To say the words, "I want peace," actually means nothing. But to mean them is everything.　ACIM, W-pI.185.1:1–2.

97　Like Dorothy in *The Wizard of Oz*, all that she had to do is click her heels together, the little ruby red slippers, three times, and say the words, "There's no place like home," to go home!　Victor Fleming and King Vidor, directors. 1939. *The Wizard of Oz.* Metro-Goldwyn-Mayer.

98　One thing you must learn about the goals the ego has given you, is that when you have achieved them they have not satisfied you.　ACIM, T-8. VIII.2:5–6.

101　There is a section in *A Course in Miracles* called "Setting the Goal" that explains that if you put the goal of peace out in front in each situation, you will perceive everything and everyone as supporting this goal.　ACIM, T-17.VI.

112　*A Course in Miracles* has nine chapters dedicated to special relationships!　ACIM, T-15–24.

113　*Each teaching-learning situation is maximal in the sense that each person involved will learn the most that he can from the other person at that time.*　ACIM, M-3.4:1.

116 *The Holy Spirit's temple is not a body, but a relationship.* ACIM, T-20.VI.5:1.

117 I let Your vision take the place of my perception, which is just a presentation of the past, appearing once again as if it's still occurring. ACIM, T-31.VIII.3:1 *Trials are but lessons that you failed to learn presented once again, so where you made a faulty choice before you now can make a better one, and thus escape all pain that what you chose before has brought to you.* ACIM, T-31.VIII.3:1

119 *Let your yea be yea and your nay be nay.* The Holy Bible, NKJV, Matthew 5:37.

124 The story of Jesus shows us how to do this. Jesus had an attitude of love and respect without people pleasing at all. He had only true empathy and true compassion. *The Urantia Book. Part IV.* "The Life and Teachings of Jesus." 1955. Chicago, IL: Urantia Foundation.

124 We are all touched by how he treated the Samaritan woman at the well... *The Holy Bible*, NKJV, John 4. (At this time Jews were not supposed to talk with Samaritans.)

124 ...and the prostitute that they caught and were ready to stone. *The Holy Bible*, NKJV, John 8:7 "He that is without sin among you, let him first cast a stone at her."

126 Jim Carrey's character in the movie *Yes Man* had to learn this! Peyton Reed, director. 2008. *Yes Man.* Warner Bros. Pictures.

131 *The mind is very powerful, and never loses its creative force. It never sleeps. Every instant, it is creating. It is hard to recognize that thought and belief combine into a power surge that can literally move mountains.* ACIM, T-2. VI.9:5–8.

137 And, if you decide to learn it, the perfect lesson is laid before you and can be learned. ACIM, M-3.5:6.

143 Holy relationship is a means to save time for yourself and the whole universe. ACIM, T-18.VII.5:2–3.

144 *Christ is God's Son as He created Him. He is the Self we share, uniting us with one another, and with God as well. He is the Thought which still abides within the Mind that is His Source. He has not left His holy home, nor lost the innocence in which He was created. He abides unchanged forever in the Mind of God.* ACIM, W-pII.6.1.

144 Mother Teresa taught this. Jeanette Petire and Ann Petrie, directors. 1986. *Mother Teresa.* Burlingame, CA: Red Rose Gallerie.

145 There is a tremendous release and deep peace that comes from meeting yourself and your brothers totally without judgment. ACIM, T-3.VI.3:1.

146 *Where two or more are gathered, there I AM.* The Holy Bible, NKJV, Matthew 18:20.

147 *Even at the level of the most casual encounter it is possible for two people to lose sight of separate interests if only for a moment. That moment will be enough. Salvation has come.* ACIM, M-3.2:6–8.

147 The way is to move beyond all concepts of attack, defense, and separate interests to the bliss and joy of this freedom, and to come wholly empty-handed unto God. ACIM, W-pI.189.7:5.

152 Because of this and of being unaware of the truth that "I can be hurt by nothing but my thoughts," the mind is actually afraid of healing, and this is why it makes itself sick. ACIM, W-pII.281.

157 And you will look with love on all that you failed to see before. ACIM, W-pI.52.

160 When the mind has full and open communication and all wrong-minded thoughts have been raised to the light, healing will follow. ACIM, T-5.V.5:2.

162 *When you forgive, forgive seventy times seven.* The Holy Bible, NKJV, Matthew 18:21–25.

164 Out of all the concepts believed in this world, forgiveness is the only truly helpful one. *Dream softly of your sinless brother who unites with you in holy innocence. Dream of your brother's kindnesses instead of dwelling in your dreams on his mistakes. Select his thoughtfulness to dream about instead of counting up the hurts he gave. Forgive him his illusions, and give thanks to him for all the helpfulness he gave. And do not brush aside his many gifts because he is not perfect in your dreams.* ACIM, T-27.VII.15.1–6.

164 *Brother, come and let me look on you. Your loveliness reflects my own. Your sinlessness is mine. You stand forgiven, and I stand with you.* ACIM, W-pII.247.5–8.

167 Forgiveness quietly does nothing. It waits and watches, and it doesn't judge. ACIM, W-pII.1.4.

167 When forgiveness is our function, we are inherently happy. Forgiveness is our key to happiness! ACIM, W-pI.121.

168 *In my defenselessness, my safety lies.* ACIM, W-pI.153.

171 For here, and only here, is peace of mind restored, for this is the dwelling place of God Himself. ACIM, W-pII.336.1.6.

171 Like in the opening scene of *Forrest Gump*, the feather is not trying to direct the wind, and likewise Forrest cluelessly goes with the flow. Robert Zemeckis, director. 1994. *Forrest Gump.* Paramount Pictures.

172 The miracle enables you to see your friend without his or her past. Let no dark cloud out of your past obscure him or her from you, for truth lies only in the present, and you will find it there if you seek it there.   *ACIM*, T-13. VI.5.

173 You will regard this person's body with its flaws and better points as well, and you will think of their mistakes and even of their "sins."   *ACIM*, W-pI.78.6.

174 Use no relationship to hold you to the past, but with each one, each day, be born again. A minute, even less, will be enough to free you from the past, and give your mind in peace to the present moment. When everyone is welcome to you as you would have yourself be welcome to God and your Self, you will feel no guilt. For you will have forgiven. *ACIM*, T-13.X.5:8.

176 *To have, give all to all.*   *ACIM*, T-6.V(A).

177 *In the state of being, the mind gives everything always.*   *ACIM*, T-4.VIII.5.

179 *I am here only to be truly helpful. I am here to represent Him Who sent me. I do not have to worry about what to say or what to do, because He Who sent me will direct me. I am content to be wherever He wishes, knowing He goes there with me. I will be healed as I let Him teach me to heal.*   *ACIM*, T-2.V.18:2–6.

181 And we shared a deep connection because it was all spoken in Matrix terms, Neo, Morpheus, Trinity, the sentinels, and so forth.   The Wachowski Brothers, director. 1999. *The Matrix*, Warner Bros. Pictures.

183 Meditation: Diving Under This World to the Light   David Hoffmeister. April 2018. "Diving Under This World to the Light." http://davidhoff meister.com/diving-under-this-world-to-the-light.

188 In this freedom is a feeling of Home. It's a presence of being home. It's a state where Heaven and Earth cease to exist as separate states.   *ACIM*, T-1.III.2.1.

190 *For a miracle is now. It stands already here, in present grace, within the only interval of time that fear has overlooked, but which is all there is to time.*   *ACIM*, T-26.VIII.5:8–9.

Internationally renowned spiritual teacher **David Hoffmeister** is a modern-day mystic and living demonstration of the non-dual path of *A Course in Miracles*. Highly inspired by Christian mysticism, Advaita Vedanta, and the desire of many to live a life of devotion, communities have sprung up around the world that follow Hoffmeister's very practical Awakening Mind teachings. His teachings are for everyone, and he spans all traditions by utilizing common ground like movies as modern-day parables and the shift in scientific theory from the Newtonian to quantum world view.

Foreword writer **Alan Cohen** is author of twenty-four inspirational books, including the bestseller *The Dragon Doesn't Live Here Anymore*, the award-winning *A Deep Breath of Life*, and the classic *Are You as Happy as Your Dog?* He is a contributing writer for the #1 *New York Times* bestselling series, *Chicken Soup for the Soul,* and his books have been translated into twenty-four foreign languages. His work has been featured on www.oprah.com, and in *USA Today, The Washington Post,* and *101 Top Experts.* Alan's radio program, *Get Real,* is broadcast weekly on Hay House Radio, and his monthly column, *From the Heart,* is featured in magazines internationally.

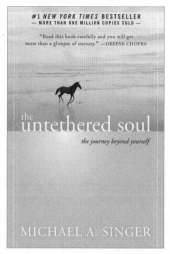
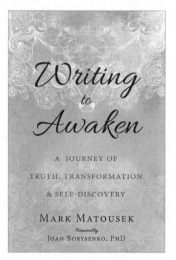
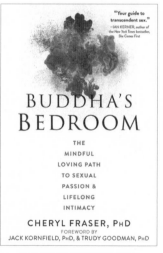

Register your **new harbinger** titles for additional benefits!

When you register your **new harbinger** title—purchased in any format, from any source—you get access to benefits like the following:

- Downloadable accessories like printable worksheets and extra content

- Instructional videos and audio files

- Information about updates, corrections, and new editions

Not every title has accessories, but we're adding new material all the time.

Access free accessories in 3 easy steps:

1. Sign in at NewHarbinger.com (or **register** to create an account).

2. Click on **register a book**. Search for your title and click the **register** button when it appears.

3. Click on the **book cover or title** to go to its details page. Click on **accessories** to view and access files.

That's all there is to it!

If you need help, visit:

NewHarbinger.com/accessories

new harbinger
CELEBRATING
40 YEARS